Sabbath
TIME

Other Books by Tilden Edwards

*Living in the Presence: Spiritual Exercises to Open
Our Lives to the Awareness of God*

*Living Simply through the Day: Spiritual Survival
in a Complex Age*

*Spiritual Director, Spiritual Companion:
Guide to Tending the Soul*

Spiritual Friend: Reclaiming the Gift of Spiritual Direction

Sabbath TIME

Revised Edition

Tilden Edwards

UPPER ROOM BOOKS®
NASHVILLE

SABBATH TIME, Revised Edition

The Upper Room® Web site: www.upperrroom.org

Upper Room®, Upper Room Books®, and design logos are trademarks owned by The Upper Room®, Nashville, Tennessee. All rights reserved.

Scripture quotations are from The New Revised Standard Version of the Bible, © 1989, Division of Christian Education of the National Council of the Churches of Christ in the United States of America. Used by permission. All rights reserved.

The publisher gratefully acknowledges permission to reprint the following copyrighted material:

Excerpt from *Prayers for the Domestic Church* by Edward Hays reprinted by permission of Forest of Peace Books, Inc., 251 Muncie Rd., Leavenworth, KS 66048.

Excerpts from *A Book of Family Prayer* by Gabe Huck, © 1979 by Seabury Press. Reprinted by permission of HarperCollins Publishers.

Cover design: Thelma Whitworth/TMW Designs
Interior implementation: Nancy J. Cole
First printing of revised edition: 2003
Printed in the United States of America

Library of Congress Cataloging-in-Publication Data

Edwards, Tilden.
  Sabbath time / Tilden Edwards.—Rev. ed.
    p. cm.
Includes bibliographical references.
  ISBN 0-8358-9862-8
  1. Sabbath. 2. Sunday. I. Title.
  BV111.3.E38 2003
  263'.3—dc21   2003000575

Contents

Acknowledgments

Special appreciation is due my family, which has supported and sometimes inspired our many family experiments with sabbath time. My children, Jeremy and Jennifer, now are grown and gone from home. I hope that the rhythm of sabbath and ministry they learned in our family will continue to feed the quality of their lives and faith.

I also extend thanks to Tom McCusker for the use of his peaceful cabin in the woods for this updated revision.

Further appreciation is due those many people in and out of the Shalem Institute whom I have had the privilege of leading on retreats and in groups, who have affirmed the need for a better rhythm of sabbath and ministry time in contemporary society, and who have helped me refine my understanding of the rhythm.

Finally I want to thank those in the Jewish community, especially Rabbis Zalman Schachter and Daniel Polish, who have taught me to appreciate the rich tradition of sabbath practice so faithfully and adamantly maintained by so many in that community.

Preface to the Revised Edition

In the middle of the weeklong residencies of the Shalem Institute's extension leadership programs, we provide a sabbath day. It's a time of protected "being time" with God and God's creation. That sabbath time consistently receives more positive evaluations than anything else that happens during the week, which indicates how strongly participants feel the need for such time in their busy lives. Here are some typical responses of people about that sabbath day:

"I have never realized God's loving presence so fully."

"I found myself appreciating everything around and in me as intimately connected with the Spirit's presence."

"I came to a deep rest, empowered to let go of my normal attempts to control life and instead just trustingly live into the moment's grace."

"I felt more compassionately connected with the people in my life and with people everywhere."

"I came to feel the fourth commandment, to observe sabbath time, as a great gift of God that ensures a sane rhythm of life."

Such responses reinforce the reasons that led me to write the first edition of *Sabbath Time* and to want to offer you this updated version. Since the first edition, the term *sabbath* has reentered mainstream Christian vocabulary, and even secular vocabulary, much more broadly. More and more people have become aware of the need for sabbath today, even if they don't know how to bring it into the normal rhythm of their complicated lives. We see signs of people's desire for a more receptive quality of time in the increasing popularity of retreats and meditation practices. However, the attempts to satisfy this need have often been erratic, unsupported individual efforts. They have not been connected with the full sense of a gifted and historically grounded corporate rhythm of life for individuals, families, and the whole church, and, in its rudiments, for all human life. Buried deep in Jewish and Christian traditions we find this rhythm of time anchored in the sabbath. Sabbath time at its heart is an opportunity for special practice of unambiguous receptivity to the free gift of life in God. This practice is meant to both balance and ground our working time. It needs to be recovered and offered in fresh forms today.

My hope in these pages is to open and deepen for us the promise of sabbath time as an integral dimension of the Christian life (as it is in Jewish life), one that touches positively all the other dimensions of our lives. I also hope that the practiced Christian rhythm of sabbath and ministry will be seen as a major contribution of the church to the whole society, one that offers an alternative to the growing societal rhythm between driven achievement and narrow escape. That deadly rhythm threatens to bury the fullness and sanity of our individual and common life and calling in God.

Finally, I hope this reflection on sabbath time in relation to ministry time will help to heal the breach often felt by people who assume that contemplation and action have nothing to do with each other. A contemplative stance to me is one that seeks to be immediately present to God moment by moment, through whatever is happening. In this sense of contemplation, separate sabbath time gives an unambiguous opportunity for our desire and appreciation for God in the moment to show themselves steadily. In ministry time, a contemplative stance also seeks to be present in the moment for God, but with special attention to how we are called to serve the world's needs and creativity in our day-to-day situations with our particular gifts. With this understanding, there is no ultimate separation between contemplation and action. If we see these two modes in terms of a fully intimate relationship with God, we could say that they find their common ground in the Gracious One who both rests and labors through us.

PART I

The Need for Sabbath Time

CHAPTER ONE

An Alternative Way

Sundays were special for me when I was young. I can remember my awe when I looked up New York's Fifth Avenue from its origin in Washington Square Park. That normally bustling thoroughfare was virtually empty and still. I crossed it every day on my way to school during World War II. But early on Sunday mornings I crossed it for a different reason—on my way to church.

Sundays left me with vivid memories: silent streets, special clothes, corporate worship that was the very center of life, and money for the church from my small allowance. After service we often shared an extended family time, frequently visiting with other families, eating especially fine food, and playing with their children in that particularly fresh way that you do with people you see only on special occasions, with the grown-ups nearby doing the same in their quieter ways.

That was a long time ago. Fifth Avenue is a lot busier now on Sunday morning. Most avenues in the Western world are busier on Sundays now. But the desire for a different quality of time from the hustle-bustle workday world has not been lost. Nearly everyone senses that work alone is not sufficient for human fulfillment.

One of the sad ironies of this situation is that, despite our intentions to allow a different quality of time in our lives, we often end up turning all our time into work time. A major reason for this is a view of reality that is reinforced by so many social forces today: a view that sees the basic reality and purpose of life as the cultivation of a separate ego needing to fulfill itself through the accumulation of many things, material and immaterial. When this is our focus, then—whether we are on a job, helping others, or in leisure time (including even prayer time)—we find that we are subtly working to produce, enhance, maintain, or protect this buildup of an isolated sense of self. This task, imposed on us by both our culture and ourselves, has an edge of anxiety and striving violence to it. We believe that it is up to us to get and to keep who we are.

This drivenness is deepened by what sociologists call the rapid shift from ascribed to achieved status in modern societies: the shift from sensing a *givenness* to who we are through family, religion, and community membership, to defining ourselves (and being defined by others) in terms of what we *produce* through whatever individual way of life this production of self and things may involve. Today we could also include what we *consume* as part of our identity: our consumption of education, material goods, public events, mass media, etc. Such consumptive activity can involve as much drivenness as our productivity.

This individualized way of life, even during leisure time, produces enormous pressure on us. When it becomes too much we are tempted to collapse into some form of oblivion: sleep, drink, drugs, television, or whatever else might numb our self-production for a while.

The rhythm of life for countless people, set up by this culturally pressured way, thus emerges as one that oscillates between driven achievement (both on and off the job) and some form of mind-numbing private escape. This crazed rhythm, based on a distorted view of human reality, increasingly poisons our institutions, relationships, and quality of life.

The churches most vulnerable to this increasingly dominant cultural rhythm are those that have been more open to cultural forces in general. These churches, at their best, for decades have held up that authentic strand of Christian tradition that looks for the Holy Spirit at work in the culture and seeks to respond accordingly. The resulting vulnerability to cultural events requires a strong, intentional basis for discerning what is of the Holy Spirit in cultural forces, and what rather is the result of collective or individual ego fears and desires, of demonic influences, or simply of innocent confusion.

Where the way of life of the people and leaders in such churches has become almost indistinguishable in intent and practice from that of any upright citizen, then the basis for Christian *discernment of spirits*[1] is seriously eroded. There no longer is an adequately distinguishable way of life that nourishes shared experiences, understanding, and disciplined attentiveness from which such discernment can be made. The result often is individual and corporate decisions and lifestyles that simply reflect the assumptions and anxieties of the larger community.

At the other end, there are more conservative churches that offer a distinctive way of life that clearly provides disciplined experiences and understanding for their people. However, these churches frequently ignore the hard task of discerning the always surprising and often ambiguous ways of the Spirit in the world, apart from what can be dealt with in simple personal terms and through rigid scriptural interpretation. My guess is that many of the people from both kinds of churches I have described, together with many church dropouts, would welcome an alternative way between overaccommodation to the culture and sectarian or inappropriate withdrawal from it.

This alternative involves the integrity of a particular way of life that is tested by scripture, tradition, and the fresh movement of the Holy Spirit in our time. It will take many forms, depending on our different life circumstances. In this sense each of us is an experiment, a unique person in a unique community at a unique time, pioneering a way of life. Yet we are experiments in continuity with those who have pioneered before us. As we seek to discern the way of life to which we are called, we need to attend to the consistencies in the way of these forebears, especially of those individuals and communities of faith that are remembered as graced bearers of God's way through human life. Christian sabbath time is one of these constants in one form or another; indeed, it could be called the historical anchor of a fundamental rhythm of time for the Christian life.

I use the words *Christian sabbath* to refer both to a special day of the week and to a special quality of time available daily. My exploration of this classical dimension of Christian life, both historically and in my own experience, convinces me that our time calls for fresh attention to it. If instead we define spiritual life exclusively in terms of ministry, then we in effect secularize rest time and leave it easy prey for our temptations to empty this time of its vital spiritual heart.

An understanding and living of sabbath time can help support a sane and holy rhythm of life for us. With it, we are given an alternative to the culture's growing movement between driven achievement and narrow escape time. Instead of this deadly rhythm, we can find ourselves in the authentic classical Christian rhythm of ministry and sabbath. This rhythm intrinsically can witness to and teach much about the Christian Way.

The uniqueness of sabbath time offers a structural and symbolic context that by its very nature resists the "works righteousness" of contemporary culture, yet without devaluing work (including service). This special quality of time can provide us with an incubator for nourishing our being in the image of God in ways that overflow into appropriate care for the world. In this way authentic sabbath time can restore the coinherence of work and leisure.

In an increasing number of Christian lives, the last vestige of the Christian sabbath is a quick hour on Sunday mornings sandwiched between the Sunday paper and a busy afternoon, and even this hour has disappeared for many. Sunday is fast becoming just another day to maintain ego focus and mastery, and to make money and spend it, in an increasingly privatized life.

Given this situation, it is difficult for us to conceive how vital and essential sabbath observance was understood to be in an earlier America and Europe. In the early nineteenth century, a naturalized American citizen from France observed that sabbath observance was the only truly American and national characteristic.[2] Voltaire, an apostle of the Enlightenment and no friend of the church, earlier declared, " If you wish to destroy the Christian religion, you must first destroy the Christian Sunday."[3] Such statements point to *the Lord's Day*, an early title for the Christian sabbath, as much more involved than a formal religious observance. Indeed, it involves a whole way of life. How we understand or ignore such a different quality of time reflects our basic theology: our understanding of human and divine nature and purpose, including the realms of work, service, play, worship, and rest.

If we are to reclaim such time and its riches in a way possible and appropriate for our age, we need to be aware of the sabbath's history as a dynamic institution, both serving and distorting the Christian Way. We should also become cognizant of the necessity of a rhythm of life for all human beings that moves between different qualities of time. A number of behavioral scientists have pointed to this reality. The only question is what kind of oscillation there will be and how much it is able to serve or muzzle full human-divine awareness and societal well-being.

One of these scientists, Bruce Reed, believes that the church's primary social and psychological task is to help people manage their experienced dependency on God in such a way that they are better able to care effectively for the world.[4] These two dimensions of dependency and caring define the needed human rhythm of life. The church is the only large-scale institution in society that is accountable for and capable of fostering such an authentic rhythm.[5] An understanding of the Christian sabbath is essential to this task.

PART II

The Sabbath in History

Hebrew Scripture

Special days and auspicious times with implied or explicit religious significance appear to be a universal human phenomenon. This points to a basic human need for a different quality of time from the daily routine of our lives so that we may recognize and live out our full humanity. Life perhaps can be lived for long periods without such special times, but only at the cost of impoverishing human awareness and vocation.

The selection of days and times in early history normally reflected human intimacy with nature. The phases of the moon, sunrise and sunset, planting and harvesting, the changing seasons of the year—each of these called for special recognition and cooperation. All mythical events celebrated on such days were seen to have been present at the origin of time, events that had no real beginning or end.

With the rise of the story of Creation and the Exodus in Hebraic tradition, we find an innovation in the human understanding of time. Historical time takes on sacred meaning. Historical events become theophanies—revelations of God. Time becomes sacred, with a beginning and end. The calendar of special days now celebrates facts that happened in history.[1]

References to the sabbath dimension of time in Hebrew scripture (the Old Testament) reveal four basic understandings of its intent. Each of these understandings has been given special weight at particular periods of Hebraic and later Jewish and Christian traditions. Sabbath has been a dynamic rather than static institution.

The Sabbath Seen As a Day of Rest

The first story of Creation in Genesis chapters 1 and 2 ends with the seventh day:

> So God blessed the seventh day and hallowed it, because on it God rested from all the work that he had done in creation.

Where this story has been emphasized in the tradition, the sabbath has been seen as a divine institution meant for all humankind.

What is meant by rest, *menuchah* in Hebrew, had a long history of development. The basic principle is found in Exodus 31:15, the commandment to abstain from any kind of productive activity. Specific prohibitions were eventually classified and elaborated by rabbinical tradition into thirty-nine categories, derived symbolically from the kinds of work involved in building the Temple.[2] The principle involved here in deciding what is work is not so much the physical nature of an activity but its *purpose*. If its intent signifies human power over nature, if it shows human mastery of the world by the purposeful and constructive exercise of intelligence and skill, then it is *meluchah*, work, that violates the restful intent of sabbath time to recognize our dependence on God as ultimate Creator-Sustainer. Here the sabbath is for God's sake, a day to be kept holy accordingly.

The story in Exodus 16:17-30 about the Israelites who gathered manna points to the *hubris* of those who continued to try and gather manna on the sabbath, despite having been given a double measure of food by God on the day of preparation that would last them through the sabbath, and despite the divine command to rest on that day. The story says that these overzealous workers found

no manna. The sabbath is for rest, in which work finds its culmi-
nation (see Exod. 20:11).[3]

The Sabbath Seen As
Commemoration of Liberation

The Decalogue is introduced in Exodus 20 with the words "I am the
LORD your God, who brought you out of the land of Egypt, out of the
house of slavery." In the fourth commandment (vv. 8-10) we read:

> Remember the sabbath day, and keep it holy. Six days you shall
> labor and do all your work. But the seventh day is a sabbath to
> the LORD your God; you shall not do any work—you, your son or
> your daughter, your male or female slave, your livestock, or the
> alien resident in your towns.

Then it continues by rooting the sabbath in the Creation story.

In Deuteronomy 5:15 this prohibition of work by any person or
animal is repeated with the justification:

> Remember that you were a slave in the land of Egypt, and the
> LORD your God brought you out from there with a mighty hand
> and an outstretched arm; therefore the LORD your God com-
> manded you to keep the sabbath day.

In these accounts we find the roots of the sabbath as a powerful moral principle of *shared* sabbath observance, a social institution
for the well-being of God's creation. Sabbath is not a private act; it
is corporate. Everything is allowed the freedom to rest on this day.
The only traditional exception is for saving life. In Exodus 23 the
land is added to this rest list in the sabbatical *year*, when the land is
to lie fallow, and whatever grows without attention shall feed cul-
tivators, dependents, and animals alike.

In Deuteronomy 15 and Exodus 21, the sabbatical year also requires releasing persons from debt resulting from loss of personal
property or freedom. Such legislation assumes that Yahweh is the

real owner of the lands of which his people are stewards. The people have it as "resident aliens" (Lev. 25:35). It is given as a conditional possession and inheritance and not for exploitation. The complaints against injustice by the prophets continued this theme, decrying a cultic sabbath detached from moral righteousness (e.g., Isa. 1:13).

The Sabbath As a Sign of Covenant

> You shall keep my sabbaths, for this is a sign between me and you throughout your generations, given in order that you may know that I, the LORD, sanctify you. . . . It is a sign forever between me and the people of Israel that in six days the LORD made heaven and earth, and on the seventh day he rested, and was refreshed.
>
> Exodus 31:13, 17

Here we find the sabbath not as an institution of God for all peoples, but as a specific sign of the chosenness of the people of Israel by Yahweh. The creation story is particularized into the creation of a people. Prophetic outcries are heard when Israel violates this unique covenant relationship (e.g., Hos. 2:11). This theme is climaxed in postexilic Israel where Ezra and Nehemiah elevate the sabbath above the law, as a special sign of the covenant people.

The Sabbath As a Sign of Hope

The travails of Israel after entering the Promised Land made it clear that the promise was not completely fulfilled. Israel did not enter into God's rest. When the land itself was taken away, the frustration was compounded. Thus Israel's prophets added the dimension of eschatological hope to the sabbath. It became a sign of promise that in time Israel would be both restored and holy. The seventh day of rest no longer was a sign of the completion of creation, but of a rest yet to be completed. Later persecutions, of course, have kept this theme very much alive.

Sabbath Practices

Hebrew scripture provides only very fragmentary evidence for sabbath practices. It is most clear that sabbath was always associated both with abstention from work and with festal activities.[4] It could be an occasion for visiting a holy man (2 Kings 4:23), or the Temple (2 Kings 11:4-12). Sabbath is associated with an attitude of joy (Hos. 2:11; Lam. 2:6; Isa. 58:13). In postexilic times the people gathered for instruction and prayer in synagogues. Sabbath rest in itself was considered an act of worship, a form of liturgy, so ritualistic prescriptions for it were quite appropriate. Postexilic Jews saw the sabbath as so special that one tradition held that on that day even the damned in hell enjoy a respite from their torments.[5]

In the Maccabean period, sabbath regulations became increasingly strict. Pious Jews would let themselves be killed rather than defend their lives on that day (see 1 Macc. 2:32-38).[6]

CHAPTER THREE

The New Covenant and
the Early Church

*I*n Greek scripture (the New Testament), sabbath beliefs and practices are taken up in the light of Jesus' words, practice, death, and resurrection.

A key phrase for understanding Jesus' approach to the sabbath is found in John 5:17: "My Father is still working, and I also am working." This close identity with God is the christological foundation for the liberty Jesus took with the sabbath (John 7:23), reinforced by the commandment of love (13:34), and his clear statement that the sabbath was made for people (Mark 2:27).[1] Jesus is Lord of the sabbath; the final rest of God will take place only after the accomplishment of the work of revelation in Christ, a work that includes the reconciliation of all creation. Then alone can there be the true sabbath rest of God. The original sabbath, along with the rest of the law, is fulfilled in Jesus' life, death, and resurrection, and yet the final eternal rest in God is still awaited in hope (see Heb. 4:9-11).

Thus the sabbath was not ended by Jesus but interpreted and fulfilled in the light of his mission. A great many of the remembered events of Jesus' life took place on the sabbath: preaching forgiveness and fulfillment of the scripture, healing and other miracles, and shared meals. On this day he also invited people to find rest in him (Matt. 11:28-30). He began (Luke 4:16) and closed (23:53-54) his ministry on the sabbath. All of this seems to point to the empowered realization of that day's covenant promise in his coming from God for a redemptive vocation.

The record does remain ambiguous, however, about the place of a special day of the week. Christ's resurrection, a number of his post-resurrection appearances, and the gathering of the disciples were remembered in connection with a new day, the first day of the week. The only Old Testament connection with the first day relates to the creation of light (Gen. 1:3-5). It was left for the early church to struggle with the relation of the seventh and first days to Jesus' mission.

Paul calls the seventh-day sabbath of the old covenant a ceremonial shadow pointing to the substance that belongs to Christ (Col. 2:16-17). He rejected the sabbath as a requirement for salvation along with the rest of the law, but he did not reject it as a body of instruction.[2] Paul gives the only directive in the New Testament about observance of Sunday in 1 Corinthians 16:2, which simply refers to putting aside money on that day for his missionary work.

Evidence for the early church's approach to the sabbath is fragmentary and varied. In general, it seems likely that the churches, comprised primarily of Jews, continued to observe a Saturday sabbath as a memorial creation, of the Christ-Logos as agent of creation, perhaps also in recollection of Jesus' redemptive ministry on sabbath days, and probably as a way of minimizing friction with non-Christian Jews. Alongside their Saturday observance they gathered on Sundays for Eucharist and an agape meal.

The Gentile church, however, at least in Rome, appears to have had no Saturday sabbath practice,[3] and the anti-Jewish bias of Roman authorities discouraged further any such practice. The first day of the week (Sunday in the Roman planetary calendar) seems to have been celebrated as the anniversary both of the first creation and the old covenant, and of the second creation inaugurated by

Jesus' resurrection along with the new life of the Holy Spirit (Pentecost also occurring on the first day).

As early as the second century, Sunday was referred to as the "eighth day," a continuation, fulfillment, and supplanting of the sabbath, both now and in future hope.[4] Eight, as Marion Hatchett says,

> is the number which transcends seven, representing the break in the closed cycle symbolized by seven. Eight symbolizes redemption, baptism, the New Age, the kairos, the fulfillment of time, the Eschaton. The liturgical week looked backward to the First Day and forward to the Eighth Day.[5]

In Revelation 1:10 we find the only scriptural mention of the designation "the Lord's day." The use of the pagan name *Sunday* was sanctioned by Saint Jerome, though he interpreted it in Christian terms: "The Light of the world rose, the Sun of Justice shone forth, in whose rays is health."[6]

The Ante-Nicene church fathers[7] were critical of the Jewish sabbath because of its pre-Christian associations and its strict observance, but they do not appear to have been fundamentally opposed to it. This view is reinforced by their strong support of the Ten Commandments. They tended to give *spiritual* interpretations to the sabbath: as the rest of heart and of conscience in Christ, as the giving up of sin on all days, as a symbol of consecrating one's whole life to God, and as a sign of future hope.[8]

The Christian *first-day* sabbath of the early church, the Lord's Day, develops into "the creation ordinance now restored to its original form to fit the gospel age of spiritual sacrifices, Christian liberty, and justification by faith. . . . The gospel takes it out of the context of elaborate legal restriction, and every Christian must be fully persuaded in his own mind just how he is to spend the day, in light of [certain] guidelines and his own situation."[9]

These guidelines included: (1) evening and/or morning public and private worship (always centered in the Eucharist); (2) acts of mercy (for instance, inviting the widows and poor to Sunday agape meals or taking meals to them, taking the Eucharist to the sick and imprisoned, and collecting money for the poor); and (3) rest. Fasting was generally forbidden on Sunday, as well as kneeling (and, added Tertullian, "Every posture of anxious care"[10]).

Sunday was not a holiday in the Roman Empire before Constantine, and many Christians could not turn it into a full day of rest. Until Constantine declared Sunday a day of rest in 321, Christians normally gathered before and after the workday: in the morning for Eucharist (and sometimes for baptisms, ordinations, and disciplines for sins), and in the evening for agape meals (followed sometimes by spiritual conversation, verses, songs, and probably prophecy and speaking in tongues).[11] Thus it was not until the fourth century that the rest of the Jewish sabbath and the worship of the Lord's Day could be fully integrated. It was also after this time that a sufficiently agreed-upon theological justification for their integration developed.

From time to time in church history, the Jewish sabbath has continued to be observed by some Christians (e.g., Seventh-Day Baptists and Adventists)[12], holding the fourth commandment and its seventh day as binding on Christians. However, the majority of churches have believed this law not to be part of the universal moral law but rather part of the ceremonial law of the Jews, freeing other Christians to shift their celebration to another day.

It should be noted here that the early church came to treat the fifty days after Easter as one long feast day. Athanasius, in the fourth century, called this period "the Great Sunday," a period prepared for by two days of fasting, a precursor to what later became Lent.[13]

Special Sunday observance was important in the early desert tradition, where hermits and monastic communities lived out the Christian Way with special intensity. This is illustrated in a story about Abba Arsenius (360–440):

It was said of him that on Saturday evening, preparing for the glory of Sunday, he would turn his back on the sun and stretch out his hands in prayer towards the heavens, till once again the sun shone on his face. Then he would sit down.[14]

The Later Church

*I*n the ways Christians regulated Sunday we see what they believed to be the good and holy life for the church,[1] as well as seeing the influence of the social circumstances of the time.

The church fathers after Constantine stressed worship and upright conduct that is becoming to the Christian on the Lord's Day, rather than emphasizing rest. This echoed an earlier dictum of Saint Ambrose, who said that Sunday should be sanctified by participation in the Eucharist and doing acts of mercy; it should not be spent on "outings" and "watching shows."[2] Growing moral laxity on Sunday led to greater weight on the fourth commandment, interpreted as keeping the Lord's Day holy. Obedience to this commandment also was encouraged through the new emphasis on the Decalogue for simple catechesis of the vast numbers of illiterate people brought into the church during the Western Middle Ages.[3] Thus the Lord's Day gradually was brought closer to the Jewish sabbath. This connection was legitimized in 789 by Charlemagne's decree, which forbade all ordinary labor on Sunday as a breach of the fourth commandment.[4] In the twelfth century we find the first known use of the term *Christian sabbath.*

Up to the fifteenth century there is no known prohibition against recreation except dancing, singing of ribald songs, theater, and races in circuses.[5] Until the Reformation the dominant view assumed that the church had the right to make such Sunday legislation, since it viewed Sunday primarily as an institution established by the church rather than instituted by God at the creation as part of universal law.

During the Reformation, Martin Luther essentially agreed with this earlier view in order to combat what he felt to be legalism in the Roman Catholic Church. He went so far as to say that, the fourth commandment being abrogated by the New Testament, no day in itself is better than another. Worship, he felt, should happen daily, but at least one day should be set aside for it, and the Sunday tradition was to be expediently followed for this, under Christian liberty.[6]

The Heidelberg Catechism of 1563 directed people to "attend church on Sunday and rest from evil works on all days" (echoing the early church fathers) and to "allow the Lord to work in me by his Spirit, and begin in this life the everlasting Sabbath."[7]

Mixed views are found in the Radical Reformation. These ranged from Saturday sabbatarians to those who held to no external sabbath, believing the Holy Spirit works on human hearts in a perpetual sabbath.

John Calvin and the Reform tradition, however, came forward with a strong position and reflected their fear of subjectivism: They came to regard all parts of the Bible as equally true and directly inspired. Calvin saw one unified covenant that included acceptance of the fourth commandment as instituted by God, expediently translated to Sunday as the day for rest, worship, and religious exercises.

Calvin himself, along with most others in the Continental Reform tradition, accepted recreation on Sunday (Calvin often bowled on Sunday afternoons). On the European continent Protestants tended to make it a half-day holiday. In England the Reform tradition went further and developed what came to be called *sabbatarianism*, a view of the divine origin of the sabbath that required it to be observed as strictly as the Jewish sabbath.

William Tyndale, considered the first Puritan, combined justification by faith with a belief in the Bible as a code of moral action, with rewards and punishments. Sabbatarianism became an integral part of the Puritan program for revitalizing personal religion and building a holy English commonwealth, a new Israel. When it became apparent that this project would continue to be thwarted by the more Catholic-oriented Church of England's view of Sunday, many Puritans translated their hopes to the American colonies, where in New England the strictest sabbaths in Christian history were developed and enforced by law, lasting well into the nineteenth century.[8]

Given the great impact of the Puritans on American life and on its Sunday practice, it is important to understand their motives at their best, and not just in their caricature as hellbent on destroying human joy and diversity. They rose out of a Britain whose leisure time (Sunday and holy days) frequently was marked by brutal sports, drunkenness, fighting, gambling, bawdy theater, and otherwise generally debauched idleness, together with selling for profit as on any other day.

The Puritans strove to bring conduct into strict conformity with the Word of God as they rationally understood it. The primary purpose of life was seen as furthering the divine purpose through our particular callings. Play was not in itself bad, but it was strictly for rejuvenation and carried the danger of luring people into sin that would lead to doubt about one's sense of assurance of salvation, since one's salvation was verified by one's outward fruits.

The Puritan Lord's Day normally ran from sunset on Saturday to sunset on Sunday, in keeping with the Old Testament tradition of beginning the day at sundown. It was set aside for public, family, and personal worship and spiritual edification, as well as for rest. It was commanded by God and was not subject to change by church or state. Holy days, not being biblically commanded, were abolished. Sometimes special separate days for recreation were declared to make up for the strictness of interpretation of sabbath rest. Special fast and feast days also could be declared. Every kind of work that could be done before or after the sabbath was forbidden. Thus, a good sabbath rest required careful advance planning (just as in an observant Jewish family). Sabbath was a time to refresh the soul and communicate its holiness to others. In its extreme seventeenth-century Scottish form, even walks, books, and music not strictly religious were banned by law in order to reinforce the sabbath's intent.[9]

For Puritans the sabbath was the fruit of the gospel, evidence of a good estate, preparation for regeneration, and an expression of the love of God. It commemorated the God of Creation and of the Resurrection, and was a foretaste of heaven.[10]

Those who did not find assurance in intellectual acceptance or external observance (for example, the Quakers) subordinated scripture to an inner authority: the direct leading of the Holy Spirit. But these dissidents observed Sunday expediently as the day for worship and rest, balanced, in good Puritan style, by six days of disciplined industry.

During the seventeenth century Jacob Boehme's spiritualized view of the sabbath infiltrated much Protestant awareness. For him the sabbath was a "type" of the eternal rest in the world to come, an abode of celestial wisdom fashioned by God eternally as a representative of his inexpressible repose. It is a day symbolizing an end of all labor and strife.[11]

The scientific revolution of the seventeenth century, with its focus on empirically verifiable laws for exploring the physical universe, began to eat away at the Puritan roots of sabbath in the immutable fiat of natural law. Puritans feared that the sabbath could not be strongly maintained on strictly expedient human grounds, and they fought to retain it, even while accepting science otherwise. The Enlightenment further challenged the sabbath in this case as a day of prayer. Benjamin Franklin exemplifies this new mentality in his use of the sabbath as a time for general study. Nonetheless, the Puritan sabbath retained much vitality and dominance in the United States until the nineteenth century, when it faced insurmountable challenges, including massive immigrations of people who held a different understanding of life and Sunday.

The great American Puritan experiment with a serious sabbath demonstrated some important strengths that we need to heed in considering a modern approach to this special time. It was a socially progressive practice that gave everyone equally a day of shared rest for spiritual awareness. In so doing, life was held up as far more than personal or social success and sensual gratification. As Winton Solberg puts it in terms of the American settling of a new land, "the sabbath guaranteed that man would cultivate the better side of his nature; wherever the sabbath flourished, people did not sink into the slough of materialism and barbarism."[12]

Another strength of the Puritan sabbath is its concern for a shared, mutually reinforcing Christian Way of life anchored in a special day. The Puritans also realized that to be maintained with any stability this sabbath requires some shared objective guidelines that transcend and inform individual subjectivism. Though the Puritan dictum that "good sabbaths make good Christians" is patently overdrawn, the loss of a collective "good sabbath" means the loss of one of the most distinctive, stabilizing, visible, and mutually supportive historical practices of the Christian Way.

Finally, the Puritan appeal to scripture as the final authority for life theoretically provided people with a powerful means of freedom from both state and church, as well as freedom from employers' historical attempts to become ultimate definers of conscience. Sabbath symbolized allegiance to a Jerusalem that is above all of these authorities. Unfortunately, however, mainline Puritans succumbed to the use of state and church to impose their own view of scripture and sabbath observance, leading to the defection of Roger Williams and many others who gave more latitude to freedom of conscience.

The defects of the Puritan sabbath focus on its legalism: its literal approach to scripture, its normal denial of Christian freedom to interpret the law broadly in relation to human situations and in response to the surprising movements of the Holy Spirit.

Its compulsory worship (not restricted to Puritans) could lead to a stultifying formalism. Finally, the Puritan sabbath tended to deny the full embodied nature of humanity sanctified in the Incarnation. It appealed only to the human rational, serious, and moral side, suppressing or ignoring the authentic nonrational (not *ir*rational), playful, aesthetic, and mystical dimensions of our nature.[13]

Anglicans and Roman Catholics (as well as Eastern Orthodox) have generally been united in affirming Sundays more as a festival than a fast, meant for the enjoyment and appreciation of God's gifted and redeemed life with all human dimensions: body, mind, and spirit. Puritan influence among Anglicans, however, and Jansenist influence among Roman Catholics, muted this festive air at times. The degeneration of Sunday festivities into various forms of debauchery further conditioned these churches' legislation concerning the sabbath. In Britain and the United States the eighteenth-century Evangelical movement and nineteenth-century Victorianism further strengthened an earnest view of the Lord's Day.

The main thrust of Anglican practice involved required worship on Sunday but with wide latitude of belief, encouragement for private religious exercises and good deeds, and rest from bodily labor (with certain exceptions, such as agriculture). Strict suppression of amusement on Sundays was opposed in the belief that God affirms the whole person and his or her need for refreshment and enjoyment of God's creation. However, recreation (and any commerce or travel) was generally restricted to afternoons, and various brutal sports were banned. The number of holy days was greatly reduced from the pre-Reformation standard, an act which, besides theological justification, had economic sanction in the need to reduce the large number of nonworking days in the calendar.

Such legislation was based on the earlier mentioned belief that the church and the Christian state have the right to provide rules for Sunday observance, since the origin of the Lord's Day was viewed as an appointment of the apostles (i.e., of the church), not of God.

This same basic view was held by Roman Catholics. Their Sunday canonical legislation evolved into these requirements: participation in the Eucharist, abstention from servile work, from judicial proceedings (following an early church rule), and unless legitimate custom or special indults[14] make exceptions, from public markets, fairs, and other buying and selling[15] (which would turn Sunday into another profit-making commercial day). *Servile work* was understood by the early church fathers allegorically to signify sin; *rest* was for freedom from sin. Therefore Sunday rest above all should be a cessation from sinful activities. Some theologians between the thirteenth and sixteenth centuries focused on the *purpose* for which a work was to be done; that is, whether it was done for earthly gain. After that period, theologians considered only the *nature* of the work. *Servile* then came to mean work that is mechanical, arduous, and physical—work that would be left to others if possible. This was distinguished from *liberal* or *common* work, which chiefly employs mental powers. That distinction has been questioned as adequate for our day, however, when some consider any work done for a living as servile and deflective from Sunday's basic intents.[16]

The Second Vatican Council reemphasized the Lord's Day as a day of freedom from work and for the community to gather for Eucharist. It gave fresh centrality to the day as "the original feast day," "the foundation and kernel of the whole liturgical year," and proclaimed joy as the called-for disposition for the day.[17]

As with Puritans, sabbath observance for Jews has been considered the *sine qua non* of their survival and affirmation of faith and identity. Its observance is carefully prescribed in the halakah, the traditional legal interpretations of Mosaic law applied to daily living. The detailed rabbinical legislation goes so far as to include protective laws that go beyond the thirty-nine categories of proscribed work to proscription of particular other conditions that are likely to lead to the desecration of the sabbath.

Despite the danger of unnecessarily burdensome legal scrupulosity, there is much wisdom in this legislation, as well as in Jewish sabbath ritual and understandings of the day, which can helpfully inform the Christian sabbath.[18] In the consistent balance of weekday Jewish social activism and sabbath rest over the centuries, we are given profound corroboration of the spiritual and social effectiveness of this rhythm, despite distortions that are inevitable in any institutionalized human structuring of time.

In the new division of the Jewish community during the nineteenth century into different communities of interpretation, we find Orthodox Jews weighting their understanding of sabbath as a witness to the authority and freedom of God's will as revealed in the Law, and to the realization that human will is most free when it conforms with this divine will.

The Reform community, on the other hand, moved toward an emphasis on the sabbath as a symbol of universal social morality and a hoped-for world of peace. As Herman Cohen said: "The Sabbath was given first to Israel. But the world has accepted it. Therefore in the Sabbath the God of love showed himself as the unique God of Love for [humankind]."[19]

CHAPTER FIVE

Erosion of the Sabbath

$\mathcal{A}$ number of developments in the last few centuries have led to our current neglect of Christian sabbath time. If we are to develop a vital and viable approach to this time today, we need to be sensitive to these realities. In the introductory chapter I referred to a deleterious rhythm of life and view of self that have emerged recently: a rhythm between driven achievement time and compensatory escape time by people trapped in a self-produced, isolated sense of personal reality. I will hold up for attention four of the many corrosive factors that contribute to that rhythm and view: American pluralism, forms of individualism, changing views of time, and the devaluation of the contemplative. As we shall see, these factors are ambiguous, for they reveal a potentially positive contribution as well.

The massive waves of immigrants who came to this country over the last hundred and fifty years came largely on different terms than the Puritans. Rather than coming with a vision of a New Israel and mutual covenant for a holy way of life, most new immigrants arrived in search of individual and family freedom from economic privation and political oppression.

The pattern of life inherited by the great number of immigrant European Roman Catholics held to a different sense of sabbath than the Puritan inheritance: a difference that focused more exclusively on worship and a festive day than on a solemn holy day of specifically religious activity. The African-American religious communities, in their own way, seemed to blend both festive and solemn inheritances of the sabbath. Each ethnic and religious group brought its own beliefs and practices. Early generations maintained their cultural and religious support bases for their own sabbath beliefs, but the new pluralistic relationships in a new land have slowly eroded these communal bases and their Sunday practices to vestiges of their earlier influence.

Of even more influence has been the restless drive toward individual well-being. The perpetual activism inherent in personally striving, competitive, production-oriented American individualism that has come to influence all Americans today—regardless of ethnic background—has made the appreciation of a reflective Sunday difficult. Sunday thus is often marked by the same hectic pace as other days, but with diversionary activity from the normal workweek. This can take the form of complex entertainments that require large investments of time, planning, energy, and money to support them. Such complex activities, in their busyness and elaborateness, can easily blot out appreciative attentiveness to divine presence and purpose.[1] I think there is a direct correlation between simple, uncrowded activities and appreciative sabbath time. Simplicity is difficult for a striving and controlling ego.

Another dimension of growing American individualism is the disintegration of identity with a common life beyond the self. This reality has been fed by the decline of ethnic communities, great mobility, and a general ahistorical sense of life. Traditional neighborhood, family, and church sharing are threatened by this increasingly private sense of life.

This individualism has its positive side as well. The strength of individual decision making and creative experiment is important in the face of collective pressures toward turning all time into essentially commercial time. Individualism also can breed respect for human differences that provide leeway for a pluralistic approach to sabbath time. Jesus again and again confronted individuals in relation to their own responsibility and differences. But this decision making and pluralism must be within a larger collective sense of mutual human-divine belonging if it is to remain true to Christian experience. Jesus pointed everyone in the same direction: toward the shared reign of God in all creation.

In a settled agricultural economy, recurrent seasons of the year have great importance, more so than any special day of the week. The larger church calendar of holy days, correlated with seasons of nature, serves such a community well. In a trading economy of migratory labor, a special day of the week is desirable: drives of herds can be relaxed, all trading can be suspended so that no trader can get ahead of another, and energies can be recreated. The sabbath rest fits well.

For an industrial-scientific economy, the all-important criterion is what the machine needs. An engine doesn't need rest, but the operator does. Operators can be staggered over seven days of the week. So human rest from labor is fine in this situation. Indeed, a growing amount of it is needed in a technologically rather than labor-intensive economy. But it is not ideal for efficient production to shut down everything for a day. The sabbath as a day for everyone can become inconvenient.[2]

Labor laws in the United States and elsewhere during the nineteenth century asserted the right of government to protect laborers from the physical and moral debasement of uninterrupted labor. These laws often went further and protected Sunday as a day of *shared* rest, so that family life and other relationships could be nurtured in a way that would be impossible if days off were staggered.

This vision has been breaking down in the face of pressures to open stores for business on Sundays, to sustain industrial production and maintenance, and to view days off in private terms.

F. W. Dillistone[3] insightfully posits two kinds of recurring and universally significant moments for people that have emerged in this modern situation: moments of *turning* and of *meeting*. *Turning* moments are the countdown/blastoff, death/life moments that come in completing particular tasks. *Meeting* moments are those birthing ones where we are involved in approaching and connecting with people. Given this situation, Dillistone believes that the church, in any celebration of time, needs to bring out vividly either the moment of supreme turning, the Resurrection, or of supreme meeting, the Incarnation.

It seems no accident that both these festivals relating to birth and death, Christmas and Easter, have retained their significance in Western lands. They are the two sabbaths of the year most likely to be celebrated. Within the weekly cycle of the Sunday Eucharist, both these motifs can be found. The Sunday Eucharist historically, in fact, was simply the extension of Holy Week and Easter into the year, encompassing the Incarnation as well.

Another view of time that has emerged in recent decades is so subtle and challenging that it has not reached popular awareness, but it is held by a vanguard of influential people. There are in fact two unlikely groups of people who through independent discoveries and radically different methodologies seem to be finding themselves bedfellows in this new view.

On the one hand are the physicists. I do not pretend to understand their evolving sense of time since Einstein. What I do understand is enough to present a challenge to our normally accepted sense of time. They bring to its logical conclusion the idea of time as being made by human hands, a conclusion that emerged symbolically with the seventeenth-century invention of the clock. Albert Einstein said that the only real time is that of the observers, who carry with them their own time and space. This leaves real time as utterly subjective. Sabbath time could only be made by humans in these terms, unrelated empirically to any foundation in the nature of things, unless it is to our innate need to carry some sense of time to order our lives, the form of which will vary from culture to culture.

This awareness is taken deeper in modern complex experiments of physical scientists. Their sense of the relativity and mystery of time seems to touch base with a very different and older tradition about which Westerners are increasingly becoming aware: Buddhism. The results of intensive meditation and analytical reflection in that tradition have evolved an experiential awareness of the coinherence of time, space, and knowledge in ways that defy our attempts to categorize them independently of one another. I, and others with me, once experimented over a period of years with a contemporary form of these practices designed to reveal this coinherence experientially.[4] For many of us it has brought a startlingly different and wondrous sense of the relation of time, space, and knowledge from that to which we are accustomed.

These discoveries (or rediscoveries) have significant implications for understanding sabbath time today. They need not contribute to its erosion, unless we ignore their relevance and fail to translate them in terms of Christian experience. We can let a sense of sabbath time symbolize the meaningfulness of our time, our history, with all its relativity, bestowed by the divine breakthroughs into our time-consciousness in Christian tradition. In this process we have an opportunity to realize what is beyond our time in those breakthroughs, that catches up our time, of which, indeed, our time is an expression: God's great time, timeless time, eternal time.

Sunday, then, is potentially an intimate realization of the coinherence of human and divine time, and an opportunity to surrender our little time to God's time for transformation. Sabbath is a structured opportunity to realize the relativity of our time in God's time. It is an intentional time to see the evidence for the trust-worthiness and hope of God's time and to rejoice in it. It is a time to realize that God's time is presenting itself ever anew through us, and mysteriously cleansing and moving our time into the fullness of God's. In this we realize that God is being timed out through and for us in every flash of a microsecond.

This concept is not easy to grasp. I am convinced, though, that these new senses of time are not in fact new to Christian tradition, though their precision of analysis is new. They express an authentic Christian firsthand awareness of reality in God through the centuries, one that for lack of a more precise term often is called *mystical* or *contemplative*. This firsthand awareness both roots and completes the moral and objectively historical interpretations of the sabbath and of Christian faith. Such a neglected mystical awareness inherently belongs to us all as creatures in the image of God. It is the awareness that provides both conceptual and affective knowledge with badly needed perspective and subtlety.

One implication for sabbath observance is the need to provide better opportunities for contemplative practice on that day both within and apart from worship. This would allow our intuitive faculty to be brought to bear for this deep realization of our subtle and mysterious intimacy with God, one another, and the rest of life. Another implication is the need to practice such contemplative sabbath moments throughout the week.[5]

If we are to reclaim a contemplative mode of mystical consciousness, which is so valuable to an authentic, full understanding of sabbath time, we need to press further into the causes of its decline. I would like to concentrate here on exposing one of its major roots: the recent history of Western ideas about the relationship of the active and contemplative life (both of which have latent mystical dimensions).

These modes of presence have an ancient history of tension and occasional reconciliation in Hebraic, Greek, and later Western thought. In Augustine we find a moment of reconciliation (though the contemplative retains an ultimately higher value for him):

> No one ought to be so leisured as to take no thought in that leisure for the interest of his neighbor, nor so active as to feel no need for the contemplation of God. . . . It is love of truth that looks for sanctified leisure, while it is the compulsion of love that undertakes righteous engagement in affairs.[6]

We find their reconciliation on a more equal basis than with Augustine's predecessors in Ignatius of Loyola, renowned for his advocacy of contemplation *in* action. We also see them together among such Reformers as Luther, Calvin, and John Wesley, wherein their new appreciation of active human callings still retains contemplative elements of worship, prayer, and faith.

But according to Robert Bellah, with Niccolo Machiavelli (who in the sixteenth century stands at the head of modern Western philosophy) we find a complete abandonment of the contemplative in favor of the analytically active. This abandonment later is reinforced by Thomas Hobbes and John Locke.

The rise of modern science dramatically brings further weight to the active life. As Eugene Klaaren explains:

> As practice and experimental knowledge gained primacy in use and value over contemplative knowledge, the very activity of knowing acquired an integrity of its own. Henceforth this activity closely approximated making or reconstruction rather than [contemplative] participation [in the known]. . . . Sharp distinctions between Creator and creation and [human] and world were also manifest between knower and known.[7]

As Robert Bellah comments, "Where God must be known indirectly through his works and not directly through participation, the very experience of transcendence is endangered."[8]

This reaffirmation of the value of the scientifically active life and capacity has brought much fruit to the world over the last few centuries, both bitter and sweet. Among the bitter fruit has been our alienation from the human capacity of participatory knowing, which historically has been crucial to awareness of our deeper nature in God. Yet we find a contemporary student of human behavior, Erik Erikson, discovering, through the very scientific tools that have aided this alienation, its detrimental quality and declaring that the mature personality expresses itself in both calculated action and contemplation. The research of Robert Bellah corroborates this finding.[9]

But such action and contemplation are not easily integrated. As Bellah comments, the "in" of the Christian attempt to be "in but not of" the world tends to collapse into the "of," just as calculated action tends to obliterate contemplation. A collective rhythm of sabbath and ministry time is one long-term means for lessening these perennial dangers.

In 1940, Jacques Maritain made an observation about American activism that gives us cause to hope that this rhythm with its contemplative dimension has great potential for clarifying and strengthening an authentic way of life:

> There are in America great reserves and possibilities for contemplation. The activism which is manifested here assumes in many cases the aspect of a remedy against despair. I think that this activism itself masks a certain hidden aspiration to contemplation. . . . On the other hand, the tendency, natural in this country, to undertake great things, to have confidence, to be moved by large idealistic feelings, may be considered . . . as disguising that desire and aspiration [to contemplation]. . . . To aspire to paradise [in American activism] is man's grandeur. . . . The question is to know what paradise is. Paradise consists, as St. Augustine says, in the joy of the Truth. Contemplation is paradise on earth, a crucified paradise.[10]

Thus we have seen the erosive and, in some cases, the potentially strengthening powers of modern individualism, approaches to time, and the dominance of an active mode of consciousness in relation to the sabbath. With this background, together with our description of the sabbath's history, we can turn now to the particular ways we might understand different dimensions of authentic and viable sabbath time today.

PART III

Christian Sabbath Time Today

Rhythm of Life

*N*ot long ago I heard an American Protestant seminary professor tell of his frustration while on sabbatical leave in Greece. Again and again he was refused when he asked for help in interpreting icons that he saw.[1] Repeatedly he was told that the only way to discover their real meaning was to sit in front of one until he understood; the icon would teach him. Or rather, God would teach him through the icon.

Likewise, we must live through the sabbath firsthand before we can understand its depths and possibilities. God can teach us through such experience. Others' words about it can provide guidelines, but we can fully understand and benefit only through practice.

Orthopraxy (right practice) is an essential complement to orthodoxy (right believing). Participation in a right way of living will teach us in a fashion that interpretive words about faith alone cannot. I am sure that such a position lay behind the answer of a Greek Orthodox theologian I once asked about missionary work. The main way Greek Christians could understand mission, he said, was to transplant a colony of Greek Christians to a non-Christian area. The implication was that their whole way of life would be the basis for attracting others. This is why attention to sabbath time is so important. It is the structural anchor of a way of life that carries its own teaching power.

Being an interpretation-minded Westerner, I think it can be valuable to share with you some thoughts that may encourage your exploration of sabbath time, backed by more knowledge about the possibilities for contemporary understanding as well as for concrete practice (in part 4).

A few years ago I was eating lunch in a restaurant on a pier in Monterey Bay, California. My attention was captivated during much of the meal by a building just outside the window at my table. It was an old, abandoned waterfront cannery, precariously held up by pilings in the water. Next door was another old cannery, but this one had been transformed into a new restaurant and store. Much modern knowledge and taste had gone into the transformation. Yet the renovation preserved the sturdy form, basic materials, and beauty of the original building.

I sensed that scene as one symbol of our time. In so many ways today we are taking a fresh look at our history and seeing what precious gold we may have thrown out or neglected in our hurry to discard the dross of the past and to assert a new way of life. Instead of tearing down particularly beautiful old structures, we are finding ways to adapt and incorporate them into our modern architectural neighborhoods in ways that draw out their enduring contributions to the landscape.

The church has been expressing this reappraisal of past experience too. Scripture and church history are being studied and mined more fully than ever for what may be there of value for us today. In the area of Christian spirituality it is clear that many people are reassessing the roots and past practices of their own traditions, as well as looking more broadly at the *whole* of Christian experience with which many increasingly identify, and sometimes beyond Christian experience.

The great danger in all this exploration is a nostalgic romanticism that ignores the ever-fresh movement of the Holy Spirit throughout history and overidealizes some particular period of experience and practice. There is no way we really can or should imitate the exact pattern of practice of another time or tradition. We should not simply reopen that romantic-looking cannery as it is. It was not built for this time. To attempt this is to betray attentiveness to the Spirit's way for us today. At the same time, it is equally dangerous to throw overboard almost everything from the past and to ignore the continuity of the Spirit's loving, challenging, creative, patterned intent in history. This intent may or may not involve continuity of many particular practices. Jesus' Paschal Mystery involved fulfillment, not destruction, of the law's intent. God's intent is steady. The practices that encourage, stabilize, and guide this intent will fluctuate in relation to the conditions of a given time. We saw this in the history of the sabbath. The church affirmed the sabbath's eternal intents of redemptive covenant-celebration, rest, commemoration of liberation, and eschatological hope for the fullness of God's shalom. But its specific form of *manifesting* these intents in particular practices has varied.

Perhaps we can see that old, yet-to-be-adequately-restored cannery as a particular symbol of the Christian sabbath today—as a neglected, still viable structure for expressing and confirming the intent of life in the Spirit, but whose particular form needs to be reconsidered in light of our contemporary knowledge and situation.

In part 3 we will look carefully at the historic intents of the sabbath as they can be interpreted for our time. This will give us a foundation for considering the particular concrete ways we might allow its viable remolding.

In the first chapter I spelled out the necessity for a rhythm of life between different qualities of time in human life, and pointed out the difference between the achievement/escape rhythm prevalent today and the intended ministry/sabbath rhythm in Christian tradition.

The rich complementary dimensions of this rhythm can be described in many ways. Over the past few years I have accumulated a list of images for these dimensions. In sharing them with you I would hope that you might be given a sense of the different qualities of mind and action that comprise our life in the Spirit, and for which differently structured time is needed. Assuring room for this rhythm is more important than the particular and varied contents we may give to the rhythm.

Note that the rhythm is between different *modes* of presence, not necessarily between different *days*. The Christian sabbath as a special day gives particular opportunity to cultivate and appreciate sabbath time. But those qualities spill over into every day, just as dimensions of ministry spill over into a sabbath day. Thus I am speaking of an intimate daily rhythm that the larger structured rhythm between sabbath and ministry *days* symbolizes and helps assure.

We find this interwoven rhythm in Jesus' life: between times for prayer, alone and corporately, and times for ministry, the sabbath observance and other days of the week. In this rhythm we see the importance in spiritual development of attending both to our relation to God and with creation (people and nature), without collapsing one into the other, even though a shared sense of life in God intimately and essentially relates and underlies them.

Put in theological terms, we have an *ontological* relationship—an essential end-in-itself relationship of being—with God that needs intentional cultivation, and we have a *moral* relationship with God that involves us in caring for life in particular called-for ways, also requiring intentional cultivation.[2] The intentional rhythm of sabbath and ministry is meant to assure their correlated attention. With spiritual maturity we see less differentiation, externality, and legality in this rhythm; indeed, we see that they live in great co-inherence. The differences are ever more clearly ones of praxis and not of underlying attitude. We see such maturity reflected in Teresa of Ávila's description of the advanced person, for whom "peace remains in the soul,"[3] and in John of the Cross's declaration that perfect balance is the result of uniting activity with passivity.[4] Each contains seeds of the other.

In our youth we normally will find great weight on the engagement/ministry side. As we grow older, there normally is more weight on the letting-go sabbath.[5] Living out of a structured rhythm of sabbath and ministry time early in life, I think, can help prepare us to be able to let go of engagement controls more appreciatively later in life when this is called for. As both engagement and letting-go modes mature spiritually, each involves an abandonment and obedience to God's way. Both are facets of one life, one ultimately indivisible reality in God.

In the following images of sabbath and ministry time, the lines between the qualities of presence symbolize their connectedness, reminding us that they do not define a dualistic reality, but rather a dialectical one: distinctions of praxis within one rhythmical flow of life.

A deep underlying attitude needs to unite these forms of presence: a single-minded, open, trusting willingness for God's will to be done through all things. When this graced backdrop is empowered, then both ministry and sabbath are saved from the fragmenting quality of willfulness.

SABBATH	MINISTRY
Open surrender	Confident action
Thank you, Lord	Lord, have mercy
Letting go	Engagement/taking on
Relaxation	Survival/coping/tension
Letting be	Seeking
Being	Doing[6]
Mary	Martha
Rachel (more beautiful)	Leah (more fruitful)[7]
Contemplative	Active[8]
Receptive	Perceptive

Sabbath	Ministry
Yin	Yang
Worship	Science
Intuitive	Analytical
Background	Foreground
Open vision	Concentrated vision
Extradependent	Intradependent
Creature	Creator
Detachment	Attachment[9]
Stability/balance	Movement/thrust
Ultimacy	Relativity
Appreciation	Management
Attention	Intention
Floating	Swimming
Sailboat	Motorboat
Integration	Dispersion[10]
Acceptance	Judgment
Simultaneity	Sequence
Ground	Figure
Eternity	History
Realized	But not yet fully
In God	Toward God
Anima	*Animus*[11]
Enjoying God	Working with God[12]
"Useless" solitude-in-community	Useful community[13]
Being known	Knowing

SABBATH	MINISTRY
Allowing	Driving
Boundless	Bounded
Root	Branches[14]
Transpersonal	Personal
Desert	City[15]
Simplicity	Complexity
Quiet prayer	Active prayer
Retreat	Pressing forward
Play	Work[16]
Peace	Conflict
Passivity	Activity
Center	Border[17]
Home	Journey
Innocent as doves	Wise as serpents
Equality	Hierarchy
Person	Role
Unity	Diversity
Compassion	Passion
Humor	Seriousness
Agape	*Eros*
Spontaneity	Calculation
Eye of hurricane	Wind of hurricane
Vertical	Horizontal
Slow	Fast
Inspiration	Expiration[18]

Sabbath Rest

Some were scandalized to find the Apostle John playing with his followers. John told one of them, who was carrying a bow, to draw an arrow: he did this several times and John then asked whether he could keep on doing it without interruption; the reply was that the bow would break in the end. John therefore argued that [the human] mind would also break if the tension were never relaxed.

—Cited from *Conference of the Fathers*, Hugo Rahner

*J*ohn understood the basic rhythm of work and rest we all need. This basic human condition is a common starting point for understanding the need for a special day of rest. But the full meaning of rest in Christian sabbath time goes far beyond this. John's play was revolutionary, not just diversionary. It happened in the context of a life lived in radical trust that God's presence is freshly empowered among us in Christ. John was truly free to play and rest, realizing that he was caught up by the work of God's redeeming power, which freed him for such times.

Sabbath rest is such a revolutionary act. It defies the boundedness of the workaday world. It witnesses to the promised messianic rest of the new creation yet to come in its fullness. It celebrates the open wonder of the Paschal Mystery rather than the tightness of personal possessions and ambitions. Sabbath rest creates a "sanctuary in time."[1] It frees us to recognize our birthright in the image of God and to resist the temptation to succumb to any lesser image. This divine image in us reveals our true dignity and source. When we cease from work, we show ourselves to be labor's master. Unlike the rest of creation that numbly spins on, we, by a conscious act of faith, can put a limit to our labor so that it does not degenerate into purposeless or compulsive drudgery. In such mastery we reflect the image of God.

In this resting time we also can realize more clearly how the creativity of our work as well as our rest reflects the image of God, and not simply our ego-image. Giving up work "lifts the veil of illusion which hides from us the true nature of human purpose."[2] We are here to live out the rest and labor of God that God alone blends perfectly: "God alone rests, not because he is idle, but because he works with absolute ease."[3]

It is because this perfection does not yet belong to us that we must create intentional times for rest, lest we forget who we are and succumb to a way of life that is narrowly enslaved to lesser powers and is generally stupefied.

Since so much contemporary life fosters such stupefaction and knows only the most shallow rest, from whom can we learn to understand the richness of true sabbath rest today?

Four sources are particularly worth attending to: *Jewish tradition, Puritan obedience, contemplative heritage,* and *the play of children.*

We have seen the Jewish roots of the sabbath and some of its more recent understandings. No people have been more attentive and faithful over time to cultivating the unique quality of sabbath. Unperceiving Christians can dismiss Jewish practice as too legalistic, too ethnic, or as irrelevant to those who trust in the new dispensation of Christ. Such people thereby sadly miss the profound, tested experience of Jesus' people with the sabbath (which he came to fulfill, not reject).

They also ignore the theological closeness of Christians and Jews (which can threaten the identities of both groups at times): Each faith tradition looks ahead with yearning to the fullness of time when the reign of God will be full. Christians believe that in Jesus Christ we come very close to the reign of God, but we also recognize that the kingdom is not yet full and awaits God's completion. The sabbath for both groups is marked by a commemoration of God's redeeming presence in history, now and yet to come, though Christians alone celebrate that presence in the Paschal Mystery of Christ. Christians approach the Law, including the fourth commandment, in the light of this mystery; the Law is not rejected in Christian tradition: it retains a gifted teaching if not a redeeming value.

Christians therefore have inadequate excuse to ignore Jewish experience and understanding of the sabbath. Such ignorance can only contribute to our impoverished appreciation of the demonstrated value found in a quality of time we sorely need help in recovering.

In an earlier work[4] I related my personal experience of living through a sabbath with a Hasidic rabbi, Zalman Schachter. His understanding of sabbath quickly dispels Christian prejudice that assumes such a day must be a repressive, legalistic burden. He says:

> There is a disease rampant—a chronic, low-grade depression that never knows how to smack its lips and say, "It's good to be alive!" It does not know the haven of a Shabbos in the bosom of an unhassling family. . . . All the nostalgia we experience is a yearning for the Sabbath—to come home to the good Mother—one's being—a homecoming with the body to the body: to eating, resting, singing, loving—resting in the bosom of Abraham. . . . The sabbath is long and full when one knows how to *be* beyond doing.[5]

Here we see classical marks of Jewish sabbath understanding: incarnate, family-based, scripturally rooted, distinguished from other times in its restfulness. Such an understanding is quite compatible with Christian understanding, especially today when the giftedness of an incarnate body is so much more appreciated by Christians as integral to God's redemption of a whole person.

A particularly valuable insight for Christians from Jewish experience is the importance of conscious withdrawal from the workaday world for a serious number of hours if any real difference is going to be realized. Jewish sabbath law aims to reconstruct the experience of Revelation wherein humans are shown their dependent, creaturely reality. This requires a withdrawal from the attitude and action of being a creator subduing the earth *(yotzer)* to one of creature *(yitzur)*.[6] "On the sabbath we lay human creative powers at the feet of God who gave them."[7]

The rhythm of Jewish sabbath ritual and other legislation aims to cultivate this shift in orientation. One rabbinical tradition speaks of the value of entering the sabbath with the feeling that all our work is completed, so that we have no hangovers from the workweek, thus leaving our minds and bodies free to be present in this different quality of time.[8]

Puritan practice, as we have seen, did take seriously a good sabbath day, consonant with their sense of the unity of old and new covenants and the viability of the fourth commandment. Perhaps the most sophisticated spokesman out of that Reform tradition in the twentieth century was the great Swiss theologian Karl Barth. He based sabbath practice on obedience to God more than on human need. This is kin to the primary historic Jewish motivation, as well, but obedience as a motivation is alien to much of modern America's culture. Thus we need to pause here a moment lest this potential basis for sabbath observance be too easily dismissed.

Obedience to conscience is supreme. But what informs conscience? In my own Anglican tradition it normally has been scripture, reason, tradition, and experience. Thus if a specific scriptural command is verified by its larger scriptural context, and interpreted positively by reason, tradition, and experience, then it calls for obedience.

In Christian Reformed and at least Orthodox Jewish tradition there has been more emphasis on obeying scripture as an end in itself, as part of a covenant commitment. For example, as a rabbi once made clear to me, a Jew does not worship in order to get something out of it, or to meet some need, but simply because worship is commanded.

Such obedience will be seen by some people as an escape from the ambiguities and responsibilities of personal discernment, escape that perhaps reveals low ego strength and high need for security. These dimensions, of course, may be present. But it is important for us to realize that obedience also can be a voluntary and mature submission of a strong ego to a particular disciplined way that is sensed as true. Looked at ascetically, it is precisely that "strong ego" that must be relativized if the deeper image of God is ever to emerge and order our lives. Obedience to a transcendent purpose—even one we do not fully understand—is a historic method of freeing us from obedience to the whims of surface ego.

If we simply do something out of love and yearning for God without trying to calculate what it will get us or even what it means, that intent and its action can carry us farther into becoming our true selves in God's image. There is a great simplicity in such obedience that can cut through much complex ego resistance to growing beyond ego-centeredness.

I am aware that an authoritarian, false religious leader can turn such obedience toward his or her own exploitative ends (witness Jim Jones in Guyana). But I think this is possible only where there is confusion between authentic obedience to the privileged Word of scripture (including its understanding through modern biblical scholarship) that grows out of a desire for attention to the deepest truth, and false obedience to another person, growing out of a sense of personal inferiority or out of desire to turn over responsibility for our lives to another human being.

The inauthenticity of the latter should not lead us to throw out the validity of the former. Such authentic obedience is one way to tame the ego-centered individualism referred to earlier that increasingly traps our true individuality in God.

Karl Barth spoke out of his authentic sense of obedience when he said:

> The command to celebrate the sabbath [is] to cease and abstain from all our own knowledge, work, and volition, even from all our arbitrary surrenders and inactivity, from all arbitrary quiescence and resting—this command claims from [us] that . . . self-understanding be radically transcended, limited, and relativized by God. . . . The command is direct to each [person]—no ethics of the holy day can come between God and the individual . . . telling him what is his obedience to this commandment.[9]

The alternative to obedience as a motivation for sabbath observance is the fulfillment of human need. This is widespread justification for the sabbath in church history. When this motivation is divorced from a sense of transcendent command, however, the sabbath inevitably loses some of its power; it is then, as Barth points out, subject to counterarguments of human need and becomes wobbly as a motivating force.[10]

Nonetheless, in our current cultural situation I think that it is primarily on the grounds of human need that sabbath practice can flourish. Along with this primary motivation, though, I hope that those of us so conditioned will consider ways in which obedience can be recovered as an ascetical value without doing essential violence to our strong valuation of personally discerning true human need and responsibility.

One of the great potential freedoms of the mature Christian life is from slavery to human impulses and wants, which gets easily confused with authentic human need. Our first need is to realize ourselves in the image of God in whatever unique vocational way is meant for us. Fulfillment of lesser human needs and wants may dull our awareness of this root need, or, we hope, sharpen our hunger for it. In either case, peace cannot come without attention to it. Sabbath observance is one form of attentiveness that melds motives of both obedience and fulfillment of human need.

What is the content of Puritan rest? Barth chides his Puritan ancestors for turning the sabbath into a bad working day in the worst sense of the word: pious exercises, forced abstentions, and regulations blotting out the real obedience called for—to celebrate, rejoice, and be free, to the glory of God. Such obedience prepares us to hear and surrender to the gospel of God's free grace, which must precede any talk of work: the law. We can't properly value and do justice to work except in light of its sabbath interruption.

The specific content of rest in Puritan sabbath practice centered on obedience to prohibitions against weekday work, along with worship, accompanied by family and personal prayer, scripture reading, and reflection. Barth adds a basic attitude toward the day: living without a program. "Let things take their course with particular freedom," in stark distinction from weekday practice. Don't radically plot or settle it beforehand. Do just as much or as little as the day brings, "without grasping after it anxiously or eagerly." The day should be free from any compulsion.[11] Barth may be a little idealistic here, especially in family or other communal setting where everyone's freedom for the day can depend on upon some agreed-upon structure, but his basic challenge to allow the day a quality of lightness is well taken.

As this lightness becomes a reality, we hope it will spill over into the workweek too, cutting into our temptations to overcontrol life willfully, and at the same time sharpening our capacity to discern those actions to which we are truly called. A light, ungrasping mind is a sharper, clearer one.

Puritans, on the whole, unfortunately do not seem to have been very good models for rest at its deeper levels (except for Quakers, to the degree they are included in this heritage). The fulfillment of

Barth's plea that the sabbath be free from any compulsion needs help from a less legal and conceptual tradition. For this I turn to the marvelous heritage of Christian experiment with rest that we find among *contemplatives*, from the desert fathers and mothers right down to contemporary Christian contemplatives, who today are often bolstered by a fresh appreciation and awareness of Asian contemplative practice.

Harvey Cox notes that the Hebrew word for God's resting used in the fourth commandment literally means "to catch one's breath." He suggests that God and people are essentially meant to do nothing but "breathe" during this time, as a source of renewal. In this way sabbath connects with certain Asian contemplative practices of just sitting and attentively breathing, as well as with related historical Christian practices.[12]

My own exposure to the contemplative heritage has been a crucial molder of rest in my life. My first conscious contact with it miscarried. It was an exposure, as a young student, to some writings of great contemplatives, without any of the personal experience behind those writings. I understood the literal meaning of their words, but not the reality to which they pointed. The words in effect were gobbledygook—a misty cacophony of obscure sounds that could not convey real sense to me. Years later I resonated immediately with the exclamation of a Roman Catholic sister in the middle of an academic course on Western mysticism she was taking: "This kind of course is just insane if you're not helped with the experience behind the concepts."

That help came for me first at a silent retreat in an Episcopal monastery. Rest was taught there more by falling into the monks' rhythm of life than by any words spoken about it. This is a mark of the contemplative way: you learn rest primarily by being given a way to experience it firsthand. Words *about* it are few. The way itself teaches, with a little help from the guestmaster. In this case the way included the classic highly structured monastic contemplative rhythm (for guests) between corporate prayer, optional times of simple manual work needed by the community, meals, and silence. Guests were let be, after a short talk with the guestmaster. He encouraged a sabbath attitude of relaxation, listening, and wasting time with God, in the building and in the surrounding woods.

Little by little I could feel the layers of drivenness and tension peel away. The structure and shared rhythm with others gave enough security and stability over the days I was there to allow me to loosen the reins of personal control; I came to genuinely rest in the Lord.

Later I learned much more precision and subtlety in such rest with the aid of a Tibetan Buddhist lama, a story I have told in an earlier book.[13] In my contemplative explorations with the Shalem Institute for Spiritual Formation over the past twenty-nine years, my sense of rest has continued to develop. I now can read some contemplative classics with a little more appreciation of the experiences behind them.

Such contemplative awareness as I have had points to some guidelines for understanding the depth implied in real sabbath rest. First we need to look at our *intent*. Why do we want to rest? We can answer this on different levels. One is the *law*. We obey out of obligation. We've seen the positive side of this motivation already: obedience can be ascetically valuable in freeing us from our own will, for the will of God. On the negative side, such motivation normally leads us only to external rest. It can become a time focused on shoulds and oughts, a kind of work that, though free of normal working activities, leaves us working inside to do the right thing.

Another motive for observing sabbath rest might be *escape*. Such rest is an opportunity to get away from something: particular people, situations, kinds of work, struggles. This motive has a positive side too: we do see the need for a really different quality of time in our life. But its negative possibility is the split mind it can produce: life is divided sharply into different realities. Sabbath rest

71

is never quite full, because there is a lurking dread that we may run into something from "the other side" that will destroy it. Also, escape can lead us to a very private sense of rest, rather than an awareness of our still being in community, still with others from the workaday world, but in a different, physically separate way.

A third motive for entering sabbath rest might be *entertainment*. We look forward to all the fine ways our bodies, egos, and souls may find enjoyment during such time. Positively, this understanding appreciates the goodness of the Lord and creation, which sabbath rest can reveal with special clarity. Its shadow side, though, is the disappointment and consequent restless turmoil that can ensue from unforeseen interferences that bring failure to these grasping expectations.

Probably each of us carries fragments of all these motives into our understanding and practice of rest. They are very human motives that we can accept without losing sight of a yet deeper one: simply shifting the focal setting of our awareness to the gospel—to the giftedness of life in the triune God's awesome, loving image. This intent for sabbath rest can lighten the moralistic temptations of the law: There is no "should" in this motive, just a realization of the way reality is at bottom. Escape is tempered by an awareness that we have not left one world for another, but rather we are attending the same integral world with the shutter of our camera eye set on infinity. There is nothing to escape; everything is before us, but from a different focal setting: one of appreciating grace hidden in everything, rather than on work to be done. Awareness of such richness in and around us also lightens our hard grasping for entertainment.

Such intent can free us to sink ever deeper into the rest of God. As this happens, perhaps we will find ourselves ever more resting in God, and in an intimate coinherence with all that is. This rest must be basically an end in itself, or work will be left in it: the work of trying for some ulterior motive—feeling good, gaining greater insight, becoming better refreshed, or whatever. Love at its deepest always is an end in itself. We want nothing more than to be present-in-love. That is enough. Rest happens in such moments. Indeed, there will be an overflow for others, but that is not the intent. "Using" sabbath time as preparation for something else, even for something good, is but another inadequate motive that will prevent full resting in the Lord.

Full rest involves all that we are; our bodies need to participate from head to toe, inside and out. Our minds and our prayers need to relax their frequent weekday grasping, striving, judging, fearing. Full rest is full openness. Full openness is God's image revealed in us: wherein all possibility, perspective, loving is obscurely realized. Such rest is a foretaste of the reign of God and its shalom. Full sabbath rest is graced rest. It is always present in potential, but we are rarely ready for it. We at least can put ourselves in its way in the quality of presence called sabbath, and be thankful for whatever loving presence is realized.

Such graced sabbath rest can appear for us in the middle of our work too, in those moments when we suddenly sense the weight of our work lighten and our striving minds become calm, leaving a quality of flowing ease, of steady self-forgetful peace through our working. Such times remind us of the underlying integration of work and sabbath rest in God's graced time.

> Unless you change and become like children, you will never enter the kingdom of heaven.
>
> Matthew 18:3

Playful mind is child's mind. It is a natural bridge between adults and children. But it is a harder mind for adults, who have that derogatory saying "mere child's play"—something too easy and simple to be bothered with.

Puritans saw how play could degenerate into debauchery and, in their fear of this, they banned play on the sabbath. Children had to give up play and be like adults. Adults had to give up this dimension of childlikeness and be serious.

There is no sabbath rest in either debauchery or heavy seriousness.

Debauchery involves an out-of-touch, mindless, careless wildness that exhausts our nervous and physical beings. Heavy seriousness clamps on tight mental and physical controls and has a way of being narrow, complicated, separating, and unresponsive to any light leadings of the Spirit. Thus seriousness too is exhausting, not restful. Any sport or other recreation that is captured by these states of mind is an escape from that authentic rest and play that reveals something of our true nature in God rather than obscuring this nature.

Eutrapelia is an old, neglected human virtue identified by Aristotle that can lend understanding to the quality of authentic sabbath play. It derives from *eutrepo*, "to turn well." It is a virtue reflecting mobility of soul, one that is able to turn to lovely, bright, relaxing things without losing authentic self in them. It is a capacity to turn deeds or words into relaxation. Eutrapelia lies between the debauched buffoon and the heavily serious boor.[14]

Freeing this virtue in sabbath time frees a quality of the image of God in us. It is that quality of end-in-itself joy that expresses the nature of God's loving, which has no ulterior motive of any kind. In Proverbs we read of God's personified wisdom:

> Then I was beside him [God], like a master worker;
> and I was daily his delight,
> rejoicing before him always,
> rejoicing in his inhabited world
> and delighting in the human race [human children].
>
> Proverbs 8:30-31

Deus ludens, homo ludens, playing God, playing man: Man/woman expressing God's image—a play free from tragic cynicism and escape, free to be "grave mirth," "grave merriment," serene abandonment to the serious play of God.[15]

The early church fathers spoke of life as a "divine children's game."[16] Ministry time in this understanding maintains a mirthful underside that can spill a quality of rest into the midst of work. In the playful dimension of sabbath time a quality of seriousness underlies the mirth, linking it to the full nature of God. Here we see the enlightened roots of the Latin title *ludimagister*, which means both schoolmaster and master of play. True play teaches us who we are and who we will be yet more completely in the fullness of God's reign. And yet the play is not ultimately for teaching; it is for being: Play simply expresses who we are in God.

Laughter is a special sign of play. Laughter can be escapist, contrived, or cynical, but not when it is God laughing through us. Then it is simply restful celebration of the life that is. Such laughter is schoolmaster too. It teaches us humility. "It notes how far all earthly and human things fall short of the measure of God."[17] And laughter is an equalizer, a leveler that deflates pretension.

Laughter also can teach us the truth. Plotinus said we truly play because of our urge to attain the vision of God, because mere seriousness does not get down to the root of things, and because a spirit of "fun, irony, and humor often digs deeper and seems to get more easily—because more playfully—down to the truth."[18]

A contemporary Kabbalistic Jewish mime, Samuel Avital, points to the opening, restful, healing physical effect of laughter:

> When you laugh, the whole system vibrates, a dancing diaphragm, dancing cells. All the cells are happy, and when you are happy you have a longer life. If you don't furnish your cells with this vibration of dancing, which we intellectually call "laughing," you are robbing them of life. So laughter is a transformer.[19]

Meister Eckhart, in one of his characteristically bold statements, plants laughter in the heart of divine creativity:

> When God laughs at the soul and the soul laughs back at God, the persons of the Trinity are begotten. To speak in hyperbole, when the Father laughs to the Son and the Son laughs back to the Father, that laughter gives pleasure, that pleasure gives joy, that joy gives love, and love gives the persons (of the Trinity) of which the Holy Spirit is one.[20]

Play is inescapable for anyone who has tasted life as essentially gifted, as an act of divine play: In creation, in Jesus Christ, in the Spirit, in all these ways God seeks to enliven what is lost or has not yet come to be. But such playfulness can be covered over in the broken confusion of the world. Sabbath time is an intentional opportunity to reclaim our end-in-itself playful divine nature.

As many kinds of restful play are possible for us as our imaginations, personalities, cultures, and the inspiration of the Spirit present. At their best they are likely to be marked by simplicity, spontaneity, harmlessness, and collaboration.

Those kinds of recreational activities that involve heavy competitiveness, great complexity, or high danger are likely to hide authentic, restful, God-revealing play. Such activities often involve too much worry, fear, heavy striving, and work for such revelation to happen. They become, in effect, extensions of work into rest time. The same mind-set is present in a different setting. Human effort is trying to make something happen. Sabbath rest, however, emphasizes trustfully relaxing into what already has happened and is happening for us in God's easeful grace.

Let me hold up one example of play, which I choose in part because it has been particularly troublesome in the church historically, and in part because it can be such a fine, shared form of sabbath play.

> We played the flute for you, and you did not dance.
> Matthew 11:17

Jesus laments the refusal of people to respond and dance to the tune his Father is playing through him.

Christians frequently have had trouble moving their bodies as well as their minds in response to life's giftedness. This reflects a number of historical realities: the misinterpretation of *flesh* and *spirit* in Paul's writings as literal physical contraries rather than different ways of being; Platonic influence reinforcing this dualism; probably early distinctions from non-Christian dancing groups; the threat of dance as equalizer with the rise of stronger hierarchical relationships in the medieval church; and fear of the distraction of authentic spirit in very sensual dancing.

Yet movement and dance receive support in Christian tradition as well. The very word chosen by the Greek fathers for the perfect mutual indwelling of the Holy Trinity, *Perichoeresi*, literally means "dancing around." Gregory Nazianzen, reflecting a number of early church fathers, affirms human dance if it is like David's before the ark: "The mystery of sweet motion and nimble gesture of one who walks before God."[21] Gregory of Nyssa said that original sin destroyed the dancelike harmony of the spirit.[22]

According to Hugo Rahner, a sacred dance of clergy and laity has been woven around the austere core of liturgy in almost every century and in countless churches.[23] Marilyn Daniels has chronicled the wide and varied use of dance by Christians from the early church until today.[24] One remarkable example was in medieval France in the Cathedral of Auxerre. There dancing followed the pattern of a labyrinth on the floor, which symbolized the church moving toward the triumph of Christ over the world's confusion. Such a dance took place in many other European churches as well.

The great Shaker song "Simple Gifts" has entered American classical folk tradition. It was sung with dancing, as seen by the words of the song:

When true simplicity is gained,
to bow and to bend we shan't be ashamed.
To turn, turn, will be our delight
till by turning, turning we come round right.

Children love to turn, to move, to dance. As body and spirit find their sacred union in the Incarnation, as we increasingly overcome their distorted historical separation, perhaps adults too, can rediscover the sabbath rest that comes in their dancing union.[25]

Such dancing involves the intent of this union, and its extension to communion with the Holy One dancing through us and all of life. This intent will produce movement in us that is different from dance done simply for escape or relief, or as another kind of competitive work. The movement may be slow, calm, and even, uniting reality in God. Or it may become fast as we are moved to relinquish our normal inhibitions with God. The movement may involve simple swaying, as is frequent in African-American church tradition. It may involve stylized movements with set patterns. Or it may rise up out of us spontaneously.

The church on the whole today is very impoverished in its expression of such movement. Where dancing is present in a liturgical or other dance group being watched, the danger is that it subtly becomes (despite its deeper intent) a form of consumer entertainment for the titillation of the senses rather than something in which one can directly participate for a different purpose: to realize the restful, ecstatic communion of what often seems broken, thereby anticipating the full dance of heaven.

Such movement certainly is not for liturgies alone. It is for any sabbath moment where we sense rest is not possible until body and spirit find each other together as one integral, reconciled reality in God, overcoming their mutual fighting, denying, or forlorn searching for one another. Such realization manifests the Incarnation, the Holy Presence for us in our full embodiment—in all that we are given.

With such intent many forms of potentially sacred movement are possible. We can absorb jogging, swimming, and endless other physical activities. We can adapt tested movements from other deep religious traditions, such as Sufi dancing, tai chi movements, and Tibetan/Indian gestures (*mudras*) of wholeness.

The key is our right intent—desiring to rise out of us whatever will assist our awareness of gifted holy communion. In such graced communion alone can we truly rest, whether realized through dance or any of a myriad of other forms of expression. Rest seen as simply the vacuum of not working is not such a sacred rest. Indeed, the anxiety of not working, of not doing anything to keep busy in producing ourselves and the world, can be far less restful than our normal working.

Stopping work tests our trust: Will the world and I fall apart if I stop making things happen for a while? Is life really gifted and the Spirit moving through it, so that I can truly rest and taste this playful caring? Can I trust that this caring will be the bottom line when I rest, beneath all the suppressed and repressed sides of myself that are likely to rise when I relax my controlling reins? Is there truly a unique image of God in me that is simply given and rises to obscure awareness in such spacious times, an image that is my deepest identity? Or is there really no such deep self in God, and does everything really depend on my producing, asserting, and protecting a conscious, managing ego-self?

The lingering doubts and confusions in us about these different senses of reality necessitate intentional sabbath rest. Such time is an opportunity to pull out of the temptation to collapse ourselves and all meaning into our self-productive world. It is an opportunity to realize our true sanity, wherein we allow trust in the Holy One living before and through us, with whom we weave a unique thread that contributes to the tapestry of the kingdom's, the divine commonwealth's, fullness.

Repeatedly I have emphasized an understanding of sabbath time that is not exhausted by Sundays.

Sundays simply are not available for everyone's rest in our complex society. Though secular labor laws still attempt to foster a shared day of rest in the week for families, increasingly this is being defeated by an ever broader range of consumer services being open on Sunday that require labor and customers. Time off on other days is given for such workers, of course, but not on a day that can be shared with family and friends: a prime motivation in secular law for protecting the same day of the week for everyone.

Even where we do find ourselves needing to work on Sundays, I think it is important to demonstrate by some special recognition our solidarity with the majority of Christians who still *can* rest that day. Perhaps that can involve shared worship; at least it can involve some special hour when we rest with special awareness of the giftedness of God's redeemed creation.

Where there is a choice of working time, I believe Christians still should seek Sunday for rest. The reinforcement of others is an important encouragement for allowing a different quality of time. Such a generally shared sabbath also helps save the day from the temptation of treating it as just a private day. Rather, at its best, sabbath is a *corporate* witness to the way Christians understand life, its rhythm, its giftedness, its meaning. Such a witness demonstrates not only solidarity with others walking the Christian Way and offering its fruits to the world, it also gives us continuity with the whole historic cloud of witnesses, back to the apostolic church, who have collectively supported one another in the Way on this special day.

For those whose free time falls on another day of the week, perhaps that day can be saved from privatism too, by treating it as a "transposed" Sunday. Such a day can be treated in the same way as the historic practice of taking the consecrated bread and wine to the sick and homebound during the week, as an extension of the Sunday shared Eucharist. This weekday rest can be seen as an extension of Sunday rest, fellowship with other Christians, indeed with all creation in intent. Such a time, whenever taken, expresses the one Rest of God that spottily touches us in this life, but someday will be fully married with labor and produce that peace wherein we, as God, "work with absolute ease."

In such an understanding of sabbath time, we are dealing not just with special days, but with those different moments of every day when *minisabbaths* come. Since these interludes so easily are blotted out in the frenzied pace of our culture, these daily times need intentionality as well. Each day can repeat the weekly rhythm of sabbath ministry in miniature. We can set aside a certain time, even if it is just twenty minutes, to still our work and rest in God in whatever ways are best for us individually, or in small households or other groups.

Such times have been institutionalized liturgically through the daily Prayer of the Hours in historic Christian tradition, rooted in the Jewish daily prayer times in which we can assume Jesus participated.

An old Hasidic saying declares that morning prayer is the sabbath of the day. In Hasidic tradition the daily prayer upon awaking was " I thank you, O ever living and ever existing King, for having returned my soul to me. Great is your faith in me." Rabbi Dovber of Lubavitch said that the first thought upon awakening has a lasting effect, setting a tone for the rest of the day.[26] No doubt such an awareness lies behind the Christian monastic tradition of being aroused with a knock on the door with some formula like "Let us bless the Lord," to which one answers, "Thanks be to God."

The different dimensions of sabbath rest we have discussed involve two stages. The first is simply *letting go*, renouncing our normal routines and work. By extension, this letting go supports sabbath time for the rest of the environment as well: other people, farmland, even machines. This is the external stage of sabbath time, one that frees us from normal demands and creates a different quality of space. Here we begin to disarm ourselves and intentionally stand more passively vulnerable, more naked before the truly Loving One.

The second stage moves beyond this negative freedom to a positive internal response. It involves letting ourselves *be* in that fresh space in such a way that we realize appreciatively and joyfully our holy connectedness.

As we have seen, this intent of rest time is different from one of escape, distraction, or chaotic sensual gratification. Realistically, though, it may well be one of these for those people whose work lives are excessively demanding and harried. There may be an inevitable period of sheer compensatory sleep and dullness before one is free to move into deeper sabbath time. Such people are likely to need a longer period of time simply to unwind from a taut working life. Two-day or longer retreats are often necessary before some of us can live into real sabbath time.

This reality of our intense times calls for regular *extensive* sabbaths for many people. Perhaps for them it will only be in such extended retreat periods of time that sabbath really moves much beyond symbolic reality. Such temporary periods of withdrawal from regular routines are common practice throughout church history (and in other religious traditions as well).

These longer periods of sabbath time can be crucial during various rites of passage in our lives: at confirmation, before marriage, the birth of a child, or the beginning of a new job (or for discerning the rightness of changing jobs), or after the death of a loved one. These are examples of those special turning points in our lives when we need a special perspective and awareness of God's grace in life, lest we miss the fullness of God's invitations to ever deeper conversion into our fully called-out humanity. These rites-of-passage sabbaths in a sense stand between our pure end-in-itself sabbath times and our functional, focused ministry times. They share the attentive rest of the former and the intentional focus of the latter. With both they share the underlying Christian attitude for all times: trust in the liberating power of God's Spirit in our midst.[27]

Churches aid the destruction of the sabbath when they misunderstand or ignore its dimension of authentic rest and in effect turn it into another busy day of work. This happens when sabbath is treated as a day of earning favors—from God and neighbor. If I go to church, God will reward me. If I help with church duties, the pastor will like me. If I bring something to the potluck supper, my neighbors will think well of me. If I, as pastor, plan many busy activities for everyone on Sunday, I am managing the church well.

Nothing is wrong with any of these activities in themselves. But if the attitude is one of "works righteousness," then Sunday becomes just a different kind of demanding day. There can be no rest when the anxiety of right work and right reward sits in the middle of our motivation. This is doubly true when we sense that the rightness of the work or reward isn't present; then our anxiety flares into guilt, fear, and anger. When such motivation is central, churches are exhausting places to be.

Understanding and cultivation of authentic sabbath rest could go a long way toward saving churches from merely mirroring the human world of the law, where there is no appreciation of the unmerited grace that frees us for holy rest. The more this appreciation is present, the more relaxed and truly joyous church activities are likely to be.

As church people begin to allow themselves to live the whole of Sunday with this attentive appreciation, they will more readily witness to reinforce a rhythm of life that realizes the truth of the Christian Way as *in* but not *of* the world, yet without falling into rigid sectarian withdrawal. Such a disciplined corporate way of life would deepen the ability of churches to offer a truly distinctive and potentially transforming way to the world.

Sabbath Worship

 $\mathcal{D}$ epth is given Christian vision not only in the sabbath rest described but also in the particular historical perspective brought to this rest. I once heard a Cistercian monk speak of his encounter with some Greek monks on Mount Athos.[1] The Greeks believed that such Roman Catholic monks had been accomplices in the pillage of Greek monasteries and churches during the medieval crusades. These monks identified with their brothers in that historical moment as if it had just happened. The Roman monk had, in effect, to do penance for that eight-hundred-year-old crime before they would fully accept him!

Such a sense of contemporaneity with all that has gone before in church history seems especially strong in Eastern Orthodox churches. That sense stretches as far back as the patriarchs of the Old Testament, symbolized in their Eastern honorific titles: Saint Abraham, Saint Isaac, and so forth. It seems no accident that these churches have maintained the strongest mystical and corporate sense of reality as well. All of historical life is presented together in the eternal eye of God. God is equidistant from the past, present, and future; as we identify with the image of God in us, we identify with the intimate contemporaneity of all events and beings in creation, caught up in the universal transfiguration of Christ.

Such a vision opens up the more dominant Western view of flat, linear time, a perspective that tends to separate past from present and future, and individual from individual, far more than the Eastern church could accept. The East accordingly might better understand those emerging views of time that I mentioned in chapter 5 than the dominant Western church (though it has been generally more difficult for the Eastern church to be open to the new in its theological and social situations).

As we approach the central act of Christian sabbath covenant commemoration, the Holy Eucharist, it is worth attending to this sense of intimate Presence brought to such sharp focus in Eastern Orthodox tradition. Amidst the fragmentation, sense of personal isolation, and alienation from both nature and history characteristic of our current Western condition, we need the strongest possible vision of the intimate, graced coinherence of life being transformed in God. This is the central witness and offering of Christian faith to our world, which is expressed in the Sunday liturgy. The whole Christian week was organized around that liturgy very early in Christian tradition.[2] Such Sunday worship is still the most visible and regularly available specifically Christian collective action.

Nothing is quite so depressing to me on Sunday than to participate in corporate worship that effectually denies this transcendent, awesome/intimate gospel witness. That denial happens in many ways:

- in sermons and hymns that shrink, privatize, moralize, over-rationalize, and divide life so that only a distorted fraction of its wondrous fullness in God is seen

- in prayers that ignore much of the world's suffering and joys, and which deal with God more in terms of our ego-wants than in terms of joining God's mysterious and trustworthy ways of loving that move beyond our narrow sense of wants

- in congregations that effectively exclude those who are "different," especially the poor

- in words that treat our ultimate personal reality as our private ego-self rather than as a unique image of God intrinsically connected with all that is

- in busy, narrow, and judging chattiness and distracted eyes, before and during the service, that can form a common conspiracy in the avoidance of interior attentiveness to the real transforming Presence within and among us

- in a tacitly ego-centered attitude of wanting to safely domesticate God and *manage* a worship service that in effect tries to secure us *from* God rather than opening us to divine guidance

- in an architectural setting that is cluttered, patched with uninspired mass-produced crosses and other ornamentation lacking the capacity to draw us through the material surface of things to the astounding mystery, beauty, and transforming power of divine presence

Thank God for the many exceptions to these services and environments. (Thank God also for the ways the Spirit sometimes squeezes through such barriers anyway!) I do not think these exceptions will be expanded simply by attacking the forms, however. Behind them lie tacit or explicit intents that produce these forms and are deeply rooted. All of us are tempted to approach worship with false intents, intents that in one way or another avoid seeing and living reality in the image of God, and instead we try to collapse God into an extension of our ego-wants. Worship can lead us to succumb to this temptation (in ignorance or hidden fear or willfulness), or worship can invite us into the gospel reality wherein we are free for celebration of our deep redeemed corporate life in the triune God.

Eastern Orthodox liturgies, for all their difficulties and complexities, have a particularly powerful way of inviting us into this celebration without so easily falling into the traps I have mentioned. In this historical moment where Christians are so vulnerable to learning from one another, particularly in spiritual practices and understanding, we can well attend to the great gift of the Eastern churches in the intent and expression of liturgy.

As with all dimensions of sabbath time, corporate worship teaches the gospel simply through participation in it. If you spend attentive time in an Eastern liturgy, just as with an Eastern icon, it will teach you. All our senses are meant to be alive in worship, not just our rational mind or our surface feelings. When, in worship, all of our senses together meet in graced surrender to God's desire to live through us, then we *know* through liturgy far more than we can talk about rationally or feel on the surface. The image of God in us is coaxed into the light, and that is through and yet beyond all of our senses.

The great Eastern contribution of a cosmic sense of God and of our own reality, so important in our time, is described by Timothy Ware:

> [B]oth in heaven and on earth the Liturgy is one and the same—one altar, one sacrifice, one presence. In every place of worship, however humble its outward appearance, as the faithful gather to perform the Eucharist, they are taken up into "heavenly places"; in every place of worship when the Holy Sacrifice is offered, not merely the local congregation are present, but the Church universal—the saints, the angels, the Mother of God, and Christ Himself.[3]

This does not express an escape from the world. Rather, it expresses the way the world *is* when we see it in God. Such worship extends the basic intent of sabbath time, to realize life in God, so that in our ministry time we may extend such transfigured life into the daily world without becoming lost in it. Non-Orthodox Christians cannot just take over Orthodox liturgy. But we can take up its cosmic intent and mold this more clearly with the particular strengths of our own liturgical heritage.[4]

One Orthodox practice we can take up more fully, however, is the use of icons—those stylized paintings of saints and biblical scenes used as two-way windows into the ever-present "company of heaven." As Timothy Ware points out, icons are placed by Orthodox not only in their churches, "but in each room of their homes, and even in cars and buses."

> These ever-present icons act as a point of meeting between the living members of the Church and those who have gone before. Icons help Orthodox to look on the saints (and angels) not as remote and legendary figures from the past, but as contemporaries and personal friends.[5]

Icons are not just subjectively inspired, as in so much post-medieval Western religious art. Their form, to be authentic, must derive from disciplined spiritual vision and understanding, which is fused (though not confused) with some subject from the storehouse of church scriptural history. The discipline of the artist classically involves being under the guidance of a spiritual director and the spiritually evolved stylistic traditions of iconography, and includes fasting, confession, and communion. The wood is blessed, the paint is blessed, and the finished work is blessed.[6] Philip Sherrard describes the result:

> [The icons'] holy personages come forth ready to bless and liberate—ready to convert the beholder from his restricted and limited point of view to the full view of their spiritual vision. For the art of the icon is ultimately so to transform the person who moves towards it that he no longer opposes the worlds of eternity and time, of spirit and matter, of the divine and the human, but sees them as united in one reality, in that unaged and ageless image-bearing light in which all things live, move, and have their being.[7]

This is the kind of powerful vision that sabbath time reveals, in and around corporate worship. Icons can be particularly helpful in unfolding the special quality of sabbath awareness.

I keep an icon (a copy of a real one) in front of me during my minisabbath daily meditation times, in a simple home prayer center, with a candle before it. The icon's image is of a Madonna and child, with the traditional gold background symbolizing the fullness of heaven. In meditation I do not look at it; I look *through* it. Looking back through it toward us, as one Orthodox monk put it, is the whole heavenly host. In that mutual gaze life is seen as it is meant to be: united in God. This is not an intellectual exercise. It is a mutual presence that comes when we release our grasping for anything, and release our sense of a hard subject-object relationship. It is an intuitive realization of our holy coinherence. From this realization, when graced, flow many blessings: repentance, true dignity, strengthening compassion, healing, or whatever else is needed in and among us.

The Russian Orthodox Archbishop Anthony Bloom says that an icon participates in "the energies of Christ," and he quotes John Chrysostom in the early church as advising us to stand before an icon and close our eyes before starting to pray. It is not by examining the icon that we are helped to pray, but simply by being in its presence, aware of God's presence of which the icon is a sign.[8]

I have seen such icons in a number of non-Orthodox churches, including that of the ecumenical Taizé community in France. They belong not just to Orthodox Christians, but to us all, as part of our common treasure in Christ. As they receive more attention, more contemporary forms of icons are beginning to evolve that reflect the same inspired, transsubjective qualities as the classic older ones.[9]

Icons draw out and prepare us for the fullness of covenant commemoration that the Sunday Eucharist unfolds. We assemble to better realize the divine redeeming acts and holy persons of history as effectively present with us now, signs of power and hope. Eucharist sacramentally extends the Paschal Mystery, the death and resurrection of Christ, through the year and through history. In its light, sabbath rest is newly possible, and we can obscurely see and trust the real history of events in their connected unfolding of God's transforming presence.

Such spiritual sight is not likely to come to distracted Sunday morning eyes that rush into an hour's worship from some other activity and plan a quick rush out to another. Corporate worship, in order to be its intended self, needs to be surrounded by a protective time zone, a time of preparation and reflection, of quiet openness with nothing to do except appreciate the presence of God in the smallest random thing in and around us. If this is done, then corporate worship is more likely to become a radiant crystal whose facets catch up all of life in God's light, placed in the midst of a velvet sabbath bed that sets it off. Without such surrounding sabbath time, worship more likely will resemble an opaque rock that reveals nothing of life's giftedness and integrity in God, only our own rushed anxiety.

Such spaciousness often seems but a remote dream to parents of demanding children and to those who have other inescapable duties before and/or after worship. For such people the intentional planning of occasional quiet days and retreats that include worship can be particularly valuable. These times can give them secured space where they can unwind and be refreshed by the hidden holy stream that is so often missed in tight daily living. If sufficient motivation and reinforcement from others is present, though, even families can find ways of more quietly preparing for worship.

When we rush through worship amidst a harried, striving day, not only do we easily miss so much of the richness and depth of its celebrative heart, but we are often left with just another flat, burdensome time of work—just one more thing to do to get through and to get right with God. We miss the liturgy's graced character. That is why Karl Barth speaks of the command to rest on this day as its real key, in the sense of renouncing our temptations to trust in our own work, and instead to surrender to sabbath rest, i.e., to truth in *God's* work. Worship is not equivalent to this sabbath command. Rather, it is a means to it.

If divine service is just another "work," then people will rightly rebel. When they grasp it as an invitation to keep to God's grace and rejoice in it, then they will cleave to the congregation and go to church on Sunday . . . where God is to be found and wants to speak to us. [We then] are guided not by whim or chance but by the Lord of this day . . . [therefore we go to] divine service not as an obligation or as part of a program, but as the natural meaningfulness, the simple thanksgiving, without which all of Sunday becomes a program.[10]

Such corporate worship, of course, is possible on days of the week other than Sunday for those who, of necessity, work on that day. Ideally, it would be done as part of whatever day off one has during the week. Such an integration with a leisured day can give perspective to the worship, and corporate anchorage to the day, saving it form the temptations of privatism that are so strong when no one else around you shares your day off.

It is easier to find formal weekday services in some churches than others. Where our own church does not provide one on our day off, then we can lobby for such a service, or go elsewhere, or organize our own informal one with others who are free on that day. If none of these are feasible, then we can at least read scripture and include a few corporate prayers of the church, both of which draw us into the church's common life, even in solitude.

CHAPTER NINE

Community

Above the bridge, we make rough camp at a cave beneath an overhang, near 14,000 feet. . . . I feel calm, and ready to accept whatever comes, and therefore happy. The turn in my mood occurred this morning, when the brave Dawa, attempting to catch Jang-bu's pack, hurled across a stream, dropped it ineptly in the water. Wonderfully, Jang-bu laughed aloud, as did Dawa and Phu-Tsering, although it meant wet clothes and a wet sleeping bag for the head sherpa. . . . That acceptance, which is not fatalism but a deep trust in life, made me ashamed.

—Peter Matthiessen, *The Snow Leopard*

Such deep trust in life is the beginning of authentic community. This graced trust, and the overflowing fruits it bears with and for others, as illustrated in this true story, expresses a basic dimension of sabbath time. In Christian experience this trust is rooted in the One whose triune image is indestructibly and redemptively present in all creation. When we authentically gather for worship, it is to celebrate this image together, that it may be realized ever more fully among us.

The stability of life's trustworthiness in God is expressed scripturally in covenant language: a covenant with all humanity given through Noah; a covenant of a particular people for all humankind given through Abraham, Isaac, Joseph, Moses, the prophets, and most especially in Jesus Christ. Gathering for worship, we celebrate a common covenant that reveals and affirms our shared double purpose in life: to rest in God joyfully and to direct the holy energy of that rest into caring for the creation with whom we share community.

We share a special bond with those who have this sense of reality together. Individual Christians do not share this in the same way: in either understanding, depth, or calling. The differences strain and break our sense of community many times. At the same time they challenge and draw out the fullness of the body of Christ in all its complementarities, sickness, sin, and blessedness.

Today we can experience this special bondedness in many places. Sociologists have long made it clear that the congregation (parish) is a secondary community for most people in our complex societies. More primary are the communities of family, friends, and sometimes of work, social service/religious societies, or prayer groups. These primary communities can often be more natural and spontaneous ones with which to gather for worship in sabbath time. For the sake of really relaxed, shared, intimate community, such bases for worship are important to cultivate. The parish church is not the only place we can gather to celebrate our covenants. If, however, we are to avoid the danger of incomplete community, of communities that develop blind spots and exclusions based on differences that narrow the fullness of covenant meaning, then we need to gather with those we have not specifically chosen to be with as well.

Parish churches often are too homogeneous, yet usually broader than the smaller communities I have mentioned. One of the great values of cathedrals is their potential for gathering very diverse people together across many different lines. Worshiping side by side with strangers gathered from many far-flung communities and parishes can remind us of the larger community that is ours to love, to learn from, to celebrate with, and to serve.

If our worship is authentic, it will reveal God's mercy. This awareness qualifies our actions on Sunday. It leads us to reflect the mercy that led Jesus to heal on the sabbath, and early Christians and the church thereafter to speak of "works of mercy" on Sunday as appropriate activities. Such works, when most authentic, are not the alienated works that come from external pressures of guilt, necessity, and demand. Works of mercy are truly *our* works, actions that come freely. These can be as simple as that curative laughter of the sherpa Jang-bu when his pack was dropped in the icy water. Or they may be planned actions that are concrete sacraments through which God's free mercy is opened to others.

Neither communal worship nor acts of mercy exhaust the community of sabbath time, however. If its dimension of rest is to be affirmed, then we need times with others when we are simply wasting time. God, in creation, wastes Holy Substance, spills expensive oil onto the feet of stars, all for the sheer playful-serious joy of it—for the expression of God's intrinsically triune-communal Being. So we can play together in sabbath time, as gods play with gods ("you are gods," Ps. 82:6; John 10:34), as images of God, joking, dancing, weaving together in expression of the one in whom all have their being.

Certainly this unity incipiently stretches beyond those with whom we share a fellowship of faith. We can playfully waste time with everyone, just as we can actively share mercy and work with everyone in our jobs and communities, knowing that we intrinsically share one Source and Hope at the bottom of our differences, however consciously veiled this may be. It is amazing how wonderfully these divine images reveal themselves among us when there is nothing we are trying to get from or give to one another. Then heavy self-consciousness falls to the ground, and the lightness of God sparkles through us. Strangely enough, to our clinging ego-consciousness, in these graced, simple, earthy, unself-conscious moments, we do not disappear as unique beings; rather, we appear as we most uniquely are, in our most given end-in-itself-ness.

We all have experienced such moments. Suddenly everyone in the room is just who he or she is, and it is all right that way. We are not judging him or her or ourselves. For the moment we are simple children of God, radiating the enoughness for now of our shared nature.

Christians sometimes forget the fuller community we share with God's creation beyond the human community. Sabbath time provides a special opportunity to appreciate our intimacy with all that comes from God's hand. Human beings have a special place together indeed, but we are inextricably bound with all sentient and created beings, from pets to plants. It is enough at times simply to be with these—just as with people—as an end in itself. This means not trying to judge, interpret, label, give, or get anything from them (though such activity may spontaneously arise). We can simply gaze through them and feel them as shared presentations with us of an overflowing Creator. Not even this need be consciously thought; to do so would retain a subtle interpretive doing. Rather, we can just allow a wordless intimate awareness, a given coinherence.

This is not easy with the pesky, poisonous, dangerous kinds of beings with whom we share this planet. There is a brokenness in creation that we all know. The wolf and the lamb do not yet lie down together. We swat the mosquito. We are wary of demons cut off from grace. And yet in a calm, trusting, sabbath mind, there is a sense of the promise that birthed Isaiah's pastoral prophecy of a peaceful creation. We accept the community that we can share now, and yearn for and somehow trust the promise of that full community of creation yet to come. In Eastern Orthodox tradition, this vision of fullness stretches even to Satan, for whose redemption one prays.

Sometimes we feel most in communion with life when we are in solitude. That paradox is expressed in the Russian word for solitude, which means "being with everyone." In the West we tend to have a split sense of community and solitude. This attitude says that if we really care about people, we will be with them almost all the time; solitude is seen as an escape from community. On the contrary, though, authentic solitude is but a different way of being in community. When our minds are not pressed by the specific demands or pleasures that come from physical proximity to others, when we are relaxed, physically alone, and aware of creation's center in God, we are not then apart from others. We are with them in a fresh way. Their images can rise before us spontaneously, and sometimes we see them for a moment more clearly as they are, minus our ego-projections. They can be appreciated, prayed for, present in a way that complements our times of physical presence.

Perhaps in such times we realize how much community is truly given us, not made by our actions. We *are* community. That is just a fact of Christian experience, though often forgotten and distorted. We can come together and recognize, celebrate, affirm, care for, and allow fresh forms of community. But we do not really have more community then than when we are in solitude, only a particular called-for expression of what we already essentially have together in the risen Christ, who reveals the unity of all.

Such an awareness can free us to let solitude live as an authentic part of sabbath time, free of turning it into escape, guilt, or a clawing sense of impoverishment. Opportunity for such solitude is a precious gift of sabbath time, which belongs to full community.

CHAPTER TEN

Social Implications
of Sabbath Time

$\mathcal{I}$n the oldest stratum of the Pentateuch,[1] sabbath is seen as a social institution: for everyone's rest and for everyone's appreciation of freedom from Egyptian slavery.[2] As sabbath understanding and practice have evolved from this foundation, a wealth of social values has emerged.

Sabbath time remembers the Mosaic covenant of statusless ex-slaves with God, as well as a new covenant in Christ of people whose only real status is given by their faith in the triune Lord of life. All who share this faith share *equality* in sabbath time. Any expedient distinctions, such as clergy and laity, are strictly subservient to this foundational equality.

Slavery and oppression by implication are violations of the way of life freely given by God, without distinction of inherited or achieved status. This awareness underlies the declaration that "He who ordained the sabbath loves the poor."[3] It also lies behind the remark that "A holiday sabbath is the ally of despotism, a *Christian* (and Jewish) sabbath is the Holy Day of freedom."[4] Despots provide holiday bread and circuses to divert the people's attention from the sociopolitical truth. Judeo-Christian sabbaths provide remembrances and signs of who we are in God's sight: ultimately equal and free from human subservience. Sabbath is presented in the Old Testament as a *right* of everyone. It was a capital offense to require anyone (or any animal) to work for you on that day. Thus sabbath is not for an elite few. It is a basic equal human right to have such a privileged time of rest. By implication this extends to the right of a daily rhythm of rest and work, and to an annual one of vacation and work. The nature of sabbath implies an understanding of justice that includes the right of equal access to the material and cultural wealth of the land, conditioned by personal need, labor, gift, and calling. It stretches beyond this common understanding of justice, however, to include the right to human unfolding and appreciation in the image of God: a religious liberty that completes justice in the framework of Judeo-Christian experience.

Authentic sabbath time implies *freedom* and invites fresh eyes and fresh breath with which to see and be in the world. We are freed from the often narrow sight and limits of workaday living. Life can be seen from the mountaintop and saved from submission to such temptations of the clouded valleys as fatalism, compulsive drudgery, rigid roles and relationships, and divisions and controls that warp, blind, and paralyze our responsiveness to the Spirit's presence.

We are free to realize our fuller humanity in the image of God that is beyond our productivity. Without this beyond, we are reduced to ceaselessly toiling beasts of burden. In this realization we give ourselves to each other more fully; each person is seen to have intrinsic value rather than merely utilitarian worth. We are free to dwell on this simple, unique givenness of ourselves and of others, rather than merely on our usefulness. We are free for a deeper quality of community.

Such intrinsic worth can be extended to the earth itself, where in sabbath time we do not seek to look at nature's usefulness, but rather its beauty and givenness with us. We can walk in the woods or park, for example, and just be appreciatively present with what is there.

An illuminating Buddhist equivalent to sabbath time exposes this opportunity of sabbath freedom. On that special day Buddhist tradition includes the practice of sleeping on the earth without a mat, symbolizing reconciliation with the earth, and eating only those fruits that are in season. Such practices are meant to assist human harmony with nature, rather than its exploitation.[5]

In returning to daily living, such tastes of sabbath freedom infiltrate the time. We carry with us some sense of a fuller humanity that maintains our dignity and promise both alone and together, beneath and through whatever work and relationships may engulf us.

In our culture, as Arthur Waskow once declared, resting on the sabbath is a revolutionary act. It is a day of "revolutionary tranquility." We liberate *time* (rather than space) as guerrilla soldiers.[6] Stopping anxious productivity for a special time challenges the assumptions of a culture that would reduce us to production machines. The quality of sabbath rest I have described challenges another temptation of the culture: to reduce us to *leisure machines*— consumers working hard to do what leisure industries tell us to do to keep us emptily busy and diverted from our deeper nature.

As we taste the fruits of authentic sabbath rest, perhaps we can appreciate the value of rest for others as well as for ourselves, and for the earth, and even for machines. We can allow the world to *happen* a little bit more easily, and loosen our grip on trying to force it to produce life artificially for us. Our productivity can take on a certain playful edge rather than the grim determination present when we see nothing but death if we cease our work for a while. The drivenness of our culture toward material wealth is loosened a bit each time real sabbath is tasted. We know an interior wealth that then leaves us full and overflowing, in contrast with the material wealth that in itself leaves us empty and fearful of loss.

We see such sabbath wealth brought to its fullness in great contemplatives like Teresa of Ávila. In her *Interior Castle* she contrasts the material poverty of the convents of the Reform and the spiritual luxuriance and beauty of our evolving life in God. Such an awareness is not an indifference to involuntary and deleterious material poverty. Indeed, all great Christian contemplatives experience renewed and active compassion as the overflow of their interior knowledge. But that overflow seeks a material sharing and expression that contrasts sharply with a view of life as satisfied by the private or corporate contrived accumulation of material goods. Rather, the contemplative overflow seeks to express in the world the joy, simplicity, equality, creativity, and loving coinherence of life in God that sabbath teaches.

In sectarian form we see this in such an early American group as the Shakers, who shaped a community of shared goods and simple beauty in their productive crafts, dress, and way of life. Such a Christian community at its best knows that its activity does not rest on seeking private possessions but on seeking God's freeing possession of us, whereby we produce stewardlike material from that cornucopia of Holy Presence.

Most of us do not live in such an integral and inspired community. We are subject to a commercial culture and its production system that rises by necessity or design from a sense of reality that easily alienates us from the intrinsic worth of the earth, people, material beauty, and God. Since, in our interdependent culture, we all share in its sweet and bitter fruits, sabbath rest is that much more crucial to give us an alternative taste of life. This taste teaches the intrinsic value of life and creation. It can feed our sane perspective of reality, save us from succumbing to alienating values, and stimulate concern for ways to be a sufficiently productive society without turning either the productivity or its wealth into idols.

The focus of sabbath time on *appreciating* rather than manipulating life offers another social value vital to our current cultural scene.

Several years ago I was struck by the way the leaders of a conference on African-American spirituality organized the time. Music, dance, poetry, and prayer lived at the center of the conference. Interpretive, analytical words surrounded these foci but did not control them, as they subtly or blatantly did in other conferences organized by dominant-culture whites (including myself) in the past. My guess is that a spirituality conference by and for Native Americans would be organized similarly to the African-American one, as would a conference organized by, for example, the Celtic Welsh in Great Britain. These three broad cultures, with all their differences, share a core of spirituality rooted in intrinsic and intuitive appreciation of life as it is sacramentally given, reinforced in each of the cultures (or subcultures) by an oppressive dominant culture.

The dominant cultures in these cases are dominant in part, I think, because of their concentration on control. The control is exercised and symbolized most centrally through concentration on rational, analytical language whose intent is to technically, impersonally understand the material and human environment in such a way that it can be controlled.

Such control has given us marvelous technological benefits. Its price, though, has been a self-feeding drive for more that does not know when to stop. Controlling language has a way of becoming a monster that spends all time multiplying itself. The mind is always whirring a grasping, utilitarian tune, even in rest time. It enslaves its owner unless an intentional halt is called.

Sabbath is such an intentional halt. It is a time for "useless" poetry and other arts; a time to appreciate a tree, your neighbor, and yourself without doing something to them; a time to praise God as an end in itself. It is a time for superfluous—overflowing the merely necessary—movements, meetings, and words. These sabbath ways check the greed of controlling mind. They relax mental reins that would drive us to dominate our neighbor and the world.

They free us from such madness so that our appreciative mind can emerge, with its simplicity and sense of God's end-in-itself presence. Our analytical, controlling mind can then be taken up again; but with a sense of its place, its stewardship of utilitarian creative powers always in a dialectical relation with our appreciative mind that values and plays with people and nature just as they are.

Our appreciative mind is colored by the myriad ethnic and personal ways we have of expressing it. Some ways are alien to us; others naturally catch us up. We can appreciate them all, however, even if we cannot participate, whenever we sense that they point beyond themselves to the God who creates life, who multiplies creation, for the sheer joy of it.

The sabbath expresses the heart of the good news, that God in Christ reveals an infinite love for us that does not depend on our works. It depends simply on our willingness for it, on our desire to turn to that great love with our deepest love, through all our little loves. Thus observance of the sabbath has an evangelical dimension. What better way to reveal God's love beyond our works than to stop our usual works and discover that love is not withdrawn but strongly visible for us? Not only is this a witness for ourselves but also for others as they see us intentionally celebrating an identity and love that is not dependent on our worthy productions. In our simple sabbath rest, doing nothing but appreciating the giftedness of life in God, we can reveal the gospel to our neighbors in a demonstrable, nonaggressive, yet very challenging way.

The forces of our society just described make it very difficult to allow real sabbath time. These are compounded by its eclipse in the church's practice. If it is to be a viable social institution, with its rich array of values crucial to contemporary society, the concept of sabbath time needs much support.

In a theocracy, we needn't worry about such support. It is given. Even in a pluralistic society we can find support within our subculture. But as society moves deeper into an atomistic individualism with no strong communal bonds, we must *invite* support. Alone, only the most gifted saints and heroes can maintain a deep quality of sabbath over a lifetime.

Parish churches and other religious communities can be invaluable in encouraging mutual covenants of support and exploration for sabbath observance. Failing this, perhaps just another person or family can be accountable with us to help ensure a rhythm of sabbath and ministry time in our lives.

If we have children, we doubly need such support. Their participation in sabbath time will likely run counter to what the ever-frenetic gang is doing on Sundays or other sabbath times. They become part of a family that is "different," just as an observant Jewish family is different on Saturdays in a Gentile neighborhood. Such difference can teach a precious capacity to *be* different, so difficult for children in a peer- and herd-oriented youth culture. This capacity, steeped in an authentic sabbath/ministry rhythm of life, can cultivate a special quality of strength, insight, and integrity that can serve society well.

The Sabbath's Ultimate Promise

*D*uring World War II a Belgian Benedictine monastery sat between the crossfire of opposing sides. While shells flew overhead, the monks continued their prayer and ordered life, just as they always had done.

Monasticism arose in the early church as communities of the "Second Baptism"—those called to anticipate in their way of life the kingdom that is to come. A number of Protestant sectarian communities later took up this call in their own way. Such communities, in effect, stretch the sabbath's peace into the week, witnessing to a way of life that looks forward in every act to the final promise, the fullness of God's reign. They sit between the world and the kingdom, pointing, working, praying, and living toward its full coming.

Their way of life, like all responses to the full sabbath's call, is subject to distortion, corruption, and incompleteness. They await grace for true sabbath living with the rest of us, but they are called to maximum attention, maximum experiment, in a way that can support that grace. They remind us all of the radical possibilities and calls of life lived sensitively and steadily in the Spirit's opening breath.

Such a way is a particular radical calling for a few people. But all Christians through baptism share in that radical calling in some way; sabbath time is a lived reminder of this calling. In such time we are meant to see, read about, experience, and reinforce regularly the roots of true life in God that are so easily covered over in the crowded cultivation time of the week. Our sights are raised to the fullest horizon of our lives; our deepest yearnings for God surface through the confused little yearnings of daily life. Hope for God's just, freeing reign is strengthened above all the frustrating limitations and despairs of the week.

Our mind's eye gives up trying to see in a mirror dimly and allows God's eye to see through us and reveal how the world can be, how indeed it will be "to faith." Vision, eyes that really see, is ours for a time. It will be tested and often blinded on the hard edges of the world and our egos as they are. But in vowed return to sabbath time the vision is restored and ever widened to include all that is real in God's eye, all that is meant to be. A discerning eye is cultivated that more easily knows the spiritual wheat from the chaff, and is strengthened to cultivate the former's deepening life in the world.

As life is seen together by grace for what it is and as it is during sabbath moments, our identity touches its bottom in God's image. In such pure sabbath flashes we no longer see through the narrow slits of ego-desire and fear. We are not ego-Christians then, who imperially protect and assert a little domain of concepts and structures labeled "Christian" over against anything that looks different. The truth of God for a moment shows its universal quality; barriers between this and that fall to a low level in the light of God's mysterious grace; we see the enormous range of that grace in human life, cultures, and nature. For a moment we are not sectarian Christians with a tribal God, but rather we are true witnesses of the universal Christ in whom everything moves and is being moved toward the fullness of God. Inner rejoicing and awe at this glimpse of the immensity of God's ways arise from the center of our being.

This awareness once was given concrete form for me in the midst of a religious-scientific conference on healing. On Saturday evening (appropriately enough) the Sufi sponsors of the conference invited a thousand people to participate in a series of "dances of universal peace." Through interwoven circles (symbols of unity), gestures, and prayers and songs in many languages, we exposed the yet-to-be-fulfilled promise buried among us. It was the very broadest welcoming of the sabbath I have known.

Such awareness and hope spills into all other times as an unquenchable flame that can light and warm the darkest, most cramped times.

These qualities of deep sabbath can emerge at any time, anywhere, but intentional sabbath time brings them to regular attention, lest they become completely buried in an ego-world whose confused ways so easily obliterate them. When we know and trust these qualities of open promise, ego itself is lightened and freed to be what it is meant to be: a vocational focusing of energy into the particular called-out ministries and sabbath joys meant for us, rather than a self-aggrandizing, protecting, isolating force out of touch with its true source and purpose. All days and times hasten toward the promise of sabbath fulfillment when our eye is graced to see through God's eye. That promise is the greatest gift of God, without whose vision the people flounder and perish.

Before moving to more concrete ways of living in sabbath time, we need to remember once more its *ultimate unity with ministry time.* Sabbath is the calm eye of the hurricane, integral to ministry time's wind, rain, sun, lightning, and thunder. They belong to each other. Sabbath, though, does not create these storms. Rather, its clear, open energy can lighten and guide them.

The daily storms of life also bring a reality check to any false sense of sabbath time. The full depths of confusion, evil, suffering, and limitation in life cut through any sentimental pious myths about life. These heavy forces need to be seen and faced as part of our human situation, together with the lighter forces: those open times of ministry when the Spirit is most invitingly present. Authentic sabbath practice is fed by our willingness to raise up all these forces to God's light. Such willingness can help bring to those forces a discerning eye that sees where and when there is graced room for our constructive movement, and where there is not. The regular perspective of sabbath practice can also help save us from too easily succumbing to these forces.

Sabbath and ministry time are united by singleness of heart: the willing of God's will in all situations and times. This graced integral will was the goal of those early desert fathers and mothers who entered the desert to do battle with the forces that divide our will, our lives, and our world from God. For us today, as for them, it is such purity of heart that we would radiate through life. Authentic, graced sabbath time gives intentional room for this heart to be strengthened and expanded.

Living a Sabbath Day

CHAPTER TWELVE

Sources and Differences

*H*ow can we concretely live through a Christian sabbath day? Individual circumstances will have much to say about the answer to this question.

Different states of life: If we are married, with young children, different possibilities and limitations are present than if we have older children, or no children, or are a single parent, or are not married and living alone, or are living in some kind of formal religious community.

Different cultures: If we are part of a Hispanic culture, for instance, we are likely to live through sabbath time differently than if we belong to an Anglo-Saxon or other culture, each of which has its own distinctive patterns of living.

Different life stages: Some research suggests that in the maturity of middle age, work and play blend together more easily than as a more self-serious young adult.[1] This attitude, and many others related to our stage in life, will likely affect how we live through a sabbath day.

Different rhythms: The times and nature of our work and that of others with whom we may live, our individual personality, conditioning, faith tradition, degree of church activity, and health, will affect how we live through the day, and even when we can live through it (e.g., if we must work on Sundays).

These differences require us to be sensitive to the impossibility of setting forth any one right way to live through such a day. Each of us will have a unique right way for the day, yet in the context of a shared intent and a shared inheritance of experience.

In this chapter I will take us through one composite way for a household, especially a family, to live a full sabbath day, drawing on my own experience and that of others. People who live alone can adapt most of these practices for themselves. Such people might invite friends and relatives to share all or part of the time with them. Even if this is not possible, though, the alone part of the day can be celebrated in conscious awareness that it is being done in solidarity with others (and incipiently with all of God's creatures).

At special liturgical times, such as Christmas and Easter, the customs would vary somewhat from those presented here, in light of the special season.

My hope is that you will find some suggestions and stimuli for going deeper into your own way. As Karl Barth says, "It is God's own affair to specify to each individual the form of the command-ment determined and proper for him [her]."[2] Thus each of us needs to go through our own discernment and experimental process, in the light of the tradition and our personal situation. If we live in community, whether that be family, friends, church, or vowed reli-gious community, we may need to go through a collective discern-ment as well.

Since I am focusing on a family's sabbath day, a word should be said about the role of parents. Mothers and fathers share a special ministerial and priestly function with the rest of the church: that of spiritual guides for their children. They are heads of the domestic church. Helping to assure and shape sabbath time for the family is a valuable dimension of their guidance. As Eugene Fisher has pointed out,[3] one lesson Christians need to learn from Jews is this special spiritual role of parents, together with the home as a center of true (as opposed to merely parachurch) liturgy. Church as exclusively *another* place with *other* leaders in our culture can turn the family into one more passive consumer unit dependent on others to provide structure, meaning, and faith.

The larger church, of course, is an essential faith-community base, support, and guide for the family, but it cannot replace the day-by-day guidance and arena for mutual spiritual struggle and discernment that the family can provide. Given the inadequate attention and support for such guidance in most communities, a family could benefit greatly from banding together with one or more other families for mutual reflection on and support of this task, including ways of living sabbath time. Single people living alone can join such a family group as well, with mutual benefit, or join with others living alone.

I will be drawing unabashedly from Jewish as well as Christian experience in this section. Just as we have something to learn from the more carefully attended meditation practices of certain deep Asian traditions (as Thomas Merton declared long ago), so we have something to learn about "shabbosing" from its oldest tradition, wherein the sabbath, indeed, has been more carefully and consistently attended to than with most Christians. When we learn from that tradition, of course, we learn in the context of Christian historical experience and faith. We cannot simply duplicate a Jewish sabbath, which would be unfair to Jewish as well as to Christian understanding. The past polarization of Christians and Jews, though, has prevented Christians from seeing how much may be truly consonant with Christian understanding and valuable for it. The great precedent for this is the significant influence of Jewish worship patterns in Christian worship historically, from the early church to the liturgical reforms of our day.

I will treat the full Christian sabbath as beginning roughly at sundown (or with dinner) on Saturday evening, and ending about sundown on Sunday evening. As mentioned in the historical section, the length of the day has varied in the tradition, with two basic patterns: from sundown to sundown, or from midnight to midnight; its longest extent (in Puritan tradition) has been from 3:00 P.M. Saturday until Monday morning. Sundown to sundown is the oldest tradition, but it may not be as appropriate for some people's situations. Experiment and adaptation are the practical keynotes of this discipline.

Approaching the Practice
of Sabbath for the First Time

The first helpful step would be your own prayer about the rightness of this practice for yourself, now that you are more familiar with its scriptural and historical values. Simply put this question before God over a period of days, and listen for what comes. If you begin to sense a particular inner peace and fullness about undertaking or expanding the practice at this point in your life, feeling that it would be a help to your presence for God, that is a sign that you are ready to take some action. It might prove to be a calling for you personally at this time, but not acceptable to your family (if you have one), in which case you need to look at how and when you personally can best take at least a part of a sabbath day for yourself, hopefully with the support of your family. Perhaps as you did this, some or all members of your family would come around in time, but whether they did or not, your sense of rightness for yourself can remain valid.

If you are a two-parent family, and your spouse is a prayerful person who you already sense would be responsive to a more intentional sabbath practice, you might begin with prayer together about this. If you sense there would likely be more hesitation or resistance from your spouse, once you are clear from your own prayer that you want to proceed, you could talk to him or her about your sense of possible calling to more intentional sabbath time. You can give your sense of personal need for such time and its possible values for the family (maybe giving your spouse a chance to read part of this book would help). You might reflect together on what weekend sabbath practices you have already felt the need for and adapted without calling them that, such as your patterns of rest, play, worship, visiting with people and so forth, along with how adequate these are, what more might be possible, what work could be given up or shifted to another day, what could be done with each other and what could be done with your children (if you have them).

You may need to give the inspiration time to steep a bit until it can be owned by both of you, at least for a trial period. If your spouse simply cannot see her or his way to be a serious part of it, then you could ask that she or he at least be supportive of you (and your children), and perhaps be involved in just one small part of it, such as the opening meal and sabbath closure. If you are separated or divorced with children, you could let your ex-spouse know what you are planning and ask for his or her collaboration in his or her time with the children, if it seems right for him or her. Single parents are often particularly pressed for time, so a more abbreviated sabbath practice may be more realistic, but just because they are so harried, carving out intentional sabbath time may be particularly important for their spiritual lives.

If you are beginning this practice with children who already have reached an age where their weekend patterns are established with a frenetic pace of activities, you will probably need to ease into sabbath time slowly and test over time how much is possible and called for together. The power of our children's friends and parents' values and patterns on our children can be very strong. You might find it helpful to try and include at least one of their friends, and ideally one or more of their parents, in some or all of your sabbath practices. If the sabbath is expressing something that belongs deep down to the nature and need of everyone, then we can hope that invitations to others to join us, after initial hesitations, will be welcomed rather than resisted as an irrelevant burden.

You might want to put the word out in your church that you feel called to experiment with more intentional sabbath time and ask for people's prayers and, if they are moved, support in reflecting on the nature of this time and possible joining you in some of its practices. You might want to talk with your pastor (or spiritual director, if you have one) about what you feel called to do, and any people he or she may know of who might be interested in talking about it with you. You may want to gather on a regular basis with others who have undertaken some intentional practice to reflect on your experience and offer prayerful support, ideas, and encouragement to one another. The church itself might want to advocate and support a period of time on Saturday nights and/or Sundays not only through encouraging some practice, but by keeping work meetings away from this time, if at all possible.

Perhaps the hardest part of sabbath for young people is its often slower, more reflective pace, away from the frenetic activities of many of their peers. Their sheer physiological conditioning to that speed may make it difficult to adapt for a long period of time. Because they are usually kept so hyped in our culture, in a way that can obliterate any spaces for God's Spirit to be recognized in their lives, sabbath time is that much more worth the effort. They can adapt for *some* period of time, even happily so if what is done remains sensitive to their capacities; how long this can be is part of the experiment for every family. You might begin by telling them something of the historic meaning and value of the sabbath, trying to hold up its positive possibilities as much as possible. You can ask them about the impact of their frenetic weekend lifestyle on their lives, how they might benefit from some sabbath practices, and what particular practice they might most appreciate.

You might outline a basic sabbath practice, such as the opening meal; going to church; some times of quiet, rest, and play during the twenty-four hours; and being together for the short closure of the sabbath. If possible, homework for Monday could be put off until after that time (Sunday night being the time most children seem to begin their homework on weekends, anyway). You might see if you can agree to experiment with a certain set format for a set number of weeks, making little changes in course as needed, and then evaluating its overall impact and how best to continue.

Teenagers present a special situation. As they struggle to gain some sense of the independence so valued in our culture, they often become less and less amenable to any but the most minimal shared family life. This is frequently less true of more family-oriented Hispanic, African-American, Native American, and other strongly ethnically identified groups, but it is especially characteristic of many older European-American groups in my experience.

Some kind of sabbath practice together can help to keep open the channels of communication and keep a sense of the family's rootedness in a divinely loved and meaningful world that transcends whatever tensions may exist together. If our teenagers are in a church youth group, perhaps sabbath practices can be discussed honestly and encouraged. Teenagers often need adults other than their parents, such as youth group leaders, to help them sort out their feelings and assist their slow transition to an adult world. Part of the asceticism of parenthood is the slow turning over of our children to others for further initiation into life (see chapter 16 for one formal way of constructively encouraging this growth passage in the church).

Realistically, then, sabbath practice in the family with teenagers may become very limited, perhaps just to a special meal and brief prayer time together, even if the teenagers once participated in a fuller practice with you. I know of one family that successfully holds the special Saturday night meal monthly instead of weekly. It might be possible for teenagers to invite over a few of their friends to share the meal with you occasionally and then remain for a low-key party together. In some family situations (with or without teenagers) a shared Saturday night meal may not be feasible at all, in which case the sabbath could be seen to begin together on Sunday morning with a festive breakfast, or the special meal could take place after church.

I do not think teenagers should be forced to participate in more than they can accept without hostility. (On the other hand, a certain vague reluctance, as opposed to hostility, may be inevitable at times!) However, with all the chaos and uncertainties in teenage life, I believe many teenagers will at least secretly value brief opportunities beyond grace at meals to touch base with a larger, stable spiritual realm at home with you.

The more casually you can simply maintain certain minimal practices together, the better; then they can just be "done," without making a big deal out of them. The price of casualness may mean that at times teenagers may not participate at all, but if certain minimal practices are maintained and normally expected of everyone, they are always invitingly present when family members are ready to return to them. Perhaps teenagers participate vicariously with some of our ongoing spiritual practices when they are not present, wanting us to do those practices for them, so to speak, during this adolescent period of peer group and individual exploration. This is one way they expect us to be a kind of steady anchor as they venture forth into new worlds in fearful, yearning fits and starts.

We need to trust that God is at work with our teens through all the turmoils of these years, wanting them to grow up and find new dimensions of their calling. Enormous and constant parental discernment is called for as we seek to trust them to God and their own evolving wisdom, and at the same time protect them from the worst dangers, evils, and foibles that they are sometimes too inexperienced to recognize.

If you are beginning sabbath observance with very young children, then you simply need to begin the practices as you are ready, keeping what you do as delightful to them as possible (such as wearing special clothes, eating special food, playing special games or other activities reserved only for this time, listening for God with them in silence for a few minutes and sharing together anything that was heard). You can let them know that you will be beginning something very special together in a few days' time, explaining briefly what sabbath is about. This will give them a period of expectancy, something to look forward to, so that when you begin they will feel more prepared.

If you are celebrating the sabbath with a spouse or someone else, or without children, what you will do together and perhaps partly in solitude during that time can be discussed between you. What you decide to do will need to be evaluated from time to time and changed, as you are moved. If you work on Sundays, you can at least recognize the specialness of the day through some brief practice and try to carve out at least a partial sabbath day whenever you have a day off.

These comments point to the reality of our complex and diverse modern living situations. Flexibility and listening for what is really called for in your particular situation are key. One other important attribute I would uphold as you read through the broad range of possibilities in the chapters ahead is *simplicity*. Trust your instincts and do only what you feel will have meaning and value for you and those with you. This is especially true in beginning the practice. You can slowly expand what you do if and as it feels right.

Preparation and Saturday Evening

Why can't we just fall into a sabbath day without forethought? If you do, you will soon discover why. You find yourself involved in many little works that eat away at the difference and rest of the day: the children have nothing clean to wear, so you must wash and iron; you're out of bread, so you must shop; you need to contact an associate before Monday about business, so you must call.

These are small examples that point to why a *day of preparation* for the sabbath is a consistently historical Jewish, and an at least occasionally historical Christian, practice. All of these examples of work could have been done the day before. No work that gives primary weight to human productivity should be done on the sabbath that can be done the day before (or after) it. If you do not follow this guideline, you likely will find your sabbath not much different from any other day, especially in the complex, hectic pressures of modern living. The sabbath needs to be as free from the usual demands and restraints as possible; it needs to provide a different space. This is the external condition for sabbath time.

Preparation for sabbath is not always easy. Extra pressure is put on Saturdays to remember all that needs to be done before Monday (or Sunday evening). If you really want to be thorough, this can include preparing for most of your sabbath meals ahead of time, as well as cleaning and shopping. These tasks can be done, as Gabe Huck suggests, with an attitude of "cleaning for renewal," and mulling over the week and letting it go.[1]

For most people Saturday is a holiday, so there is time to sort out what is essential and do it. The rewards of a real sabbath day are more than worth the effort (if you need more than the fourth commandment for motivation). Roger Beckwith reminds us that we normally need to *share* whatever work has to be done for the sabbath (either in preparation or, where necessary, on the sabbath itself), so no one person (or gender) has all of it.[2] Such sharing can also assist a family's solidarity.

A layman I know has developed a somewhat different way of relating Saturday and Sunday that I would hold up as an option for those who do not need much time for preparatory work. He uses the historic Jewish sabbath, Saturday, as a time of devotion, study, and prayer. For him this cultivates a Christian Sunday sabbath as a real celebration of joy and praise. As he puts it, "Saturday becomes a day of preparation and Sunday a day of expression." In the composite picture of sabbath possibilities I am elaborating, some of this man's practices are telescoped into my description of Saturday evenings.

Saturday Evening

Dinner is ready. Each person may be wearing something special. Three candles are lit with a blessing, one for each of the ways God comes to us in Christian experience—as Creator, Redeemer, and Inspirer—or a candle may be lit for each member of the family. Then the children are blessed. Either here or after dinner the family reads together a psalm, followed by an expression of praise to the triune God who gives us this sabbath and this life.

Next, those gathered turn toward the open door and welcome the Sabbath Queen, who lives with us for this special day. Following a brief song of welcome, we bless God over wine (or grape juice) and bread, then sit down to a special meal. Dinner ends with a thanksgiving, after which we let the sabbath's peace and freedom reign as opportunity presents.

At the end of the evening we take our baths (if we haven't done this as part of preparation for sabbath) with a special sense of memory: the creative, cleansing, renewing power of God through water in the biblical stories of Creation, the Flood, and the Exodus; and in our baptism. Prayers are said with the children before bed and include special thanksgiving and petition for the peace of this sabbath day.

Whatever is done to open the sabbath, the importance of the opening ritual needs to be emphasized. A ritualized transition to the sabbath day helps free us to live into the difference of sabbath time. Even in a secular context of work and rest, recent research has shown that many people develop "leisure sickness," with physical symptoms such as headaches and fatigue, when they cannot make the transition from a work to a nonwork environment. A ritualized bridging into the different reality and meaningfulness of the sabbath can help to counter this human difficulty.[3]

Let me go back to the beginning of the evening now and provide a little more understanding and detail of some of many possible ingredients for opening the sabbath.

Clothes

Special clothes for Sunday is an old custom that recently has been falling into neglect, under the combined pressures of more informal lifestyles and the more subtle pressure of a culture that less and less sees any time as very special, compared with past historical periods. Special clothes certainly are not necessary for a good sabbath, but they can reinforce its sense of difference.

Special dress can range from a complete outfit set aside strictly for the sabbath to merely a special pin, flower, or single piece of clothing that sets off the time. Such dress will be least distracting and most helpful if it is both simple and, for us, beautiful—not something to show off, but to express the simple beauty of the sabbath. When we all come together for the first sabbath meal wearing something special, we reinforce the celebrative atmosphere for ourselves and for one another. The gathering has a different feel to it than if we come in the T-shirt and jeans in which we've just mowed the lawn or played ball. Perhaps we might sense a bit more our own and each other's unique collective dignity in the eyes of God in this symbolic way.

Special clothing can be extended to the dining table as well: perhaps a special tablecloth and napkins, special plates and silverware, if these are to be had, and flowers.

Candles

The lighting of candles (by the mother in Jewish tradition) connects us not only with ancient Jewish sabbath tradition, but with the early Christian custom of lighting the lamp at a Saturday or Sunday evening meal, with a blessing of God the giver of light, especially the light of Christ.[4]

The ancient Greek hymn "O Gladsome Light," still found in some modern hymnals, was often sung at this time in the early church, a practice that some may well want to include at this time.

There is nothing sacred or particularly traditional about lighting three candles instead of one, two, or any other number. However, I find that three, in recollection of the triune God at the heart of Christian faith and experience, is a symbolically powerful way of expressing this reality. Where children are present, this has subliminal instructional value as well. The flame itself is the most important symbol. It is an open image of God that carries us beyond any fumbling, finite interpretive words about God with which we might surround it.

Some people may prefer the Jewish custom of lighting a candle for each member of the family. This has the symbolic power of recognizing every person as having a special place in this unit of God's family, and seeing every person as an extension of God's light in the world.

Another Jewish tradition would see two candles lit, to point out that when we enter sabbath, the flames of God and self are separate, as opposed to how the flames will be when sabbath ends. Also in Jewish tradition the right hand is waved over the flame three times to usher in the spirit of sabbath. Then eyes are closed, or hands are put over the eyes, to shield them from the light. One Jewish person I know loves opening her eyes afterward and thinking that the light has been there all along, just waiting for her to see it.

The practice of beginning the Christian sabbath with candle lighting also exists today in a number of formal religious communities, such as the ecumenical Taizé community in France and the Anglican Franciscans in Dorset, England. In these particular communities the members kneel around the altar in darkness and silence for a few minutes. Then a candle is slowly borne into the midst of the sanctuary by one of the brothers, who lights the gospel candle at the lectern. Next the head of the community takes a light from this candle and gives it to the first person, who proceeds to light the altar candles and the votive lamps in front of the sacred icons. Then a spotlight is turned onto the central crucifix, and all the house lights slowly follow. In this way a new day, a new week, a new sabbath, a "little Easter" is proclaimed.[5]

An adaptation of this practice is possible in a family setting, using the table as the altar. Some families and individuals may want to gather in the church together for such a sabbath opening on the eve of certain sabbaths, as indeed many do by tradition on Christmas and Easter eves.

Gabe Huck, borrowing from Jewish tradition, suggests the following ritual as the candles are lit:

All standing, one person or all say:

> Come, let us welcome the sabbath.
> May its radiance illumine our hearts as we kindle
>   these tapers.[6]

Then, looking at the lights, all may pray silently for one another. After this the one who lit the candles concludes:

> May the Lord bless us with sabbath joy.
> May the Lord bless us with sabbath holiness.
> May the Lord bless us with sabbath peace.

Ed Hays suggests an alternative opening:

Light is the sacrament of God's Presence among us.
The Lord is our Light and our Salvation.
We are called to be the children of light,
    to be a light unto all nations.
Blessed are you, Lord our God,
    who has made us light to one another.
In the spirit of our ancient traditions,
    we now light these festive meal candles. . . .
May our home be made holy, O God, by your Light.
May the light of Love and Truth shine upon us all
    as a blessing from you.
May our table and our family
be consecrated by your Divine Presence
    at this meal and at all our family meals.
Amen.

Come,
Let us welcome this first day of a new week: Sunday.
On this day, our Lord Jesus Christ
    did rise from the darkness of the tomb.
This meal brings blessing to our hearts
    as our workday thoughts and toils
    are forgotten.[7]

Still another possible prayer over the candles is this:

> May the light of the sabbath candles drive out from among us the spirit of anger and the spirit of fear. Send your blessing that we may walk in the ways of your Word and your Light. Enter our hearts this night.[8]

In Jewish tradition, the woman who lights the candles will make a gesture over the flame with her hands of bringing the holy light of God closer, symbolizing her hope for the deeper penetration of that light into herself and her family. Perhaps everyone observing this opening of the sabbath could participate in this gesture together, along with sharing the prayer for God's blessing.

Blessing Children

Another important ritual from Jewish tradition is the blessing of children at this time. I heartily concur with Huck's encouragement of this practice. It strongly reinforces the adult role of priestly and spiritual guidance of children, which is missing from so many Christian homes. Parents and other adults place a hand in blessing on the heads of children, and one prays this (or some other) blessing:

> The Lord bless you and keep you;
> the Lord make his face to shine upon you,
>   and be gracious to you;
> the Lord lift up his countenance upon you,
>   and give you peace.
>   Numbers 6:24-26

Such a blessing, with its physical touch and special intercession for the child, can be very reassuring. It concretely connects the child with God's grace, and with parents and other adults as potential channels of that grace. For the adults, it reminds them of this transcendent and privileged dimension of their parental stewardship.

I know one mother who extended such a formal blessing to her four children before they left for school each day, as well as in sickness and on other occasions. When they were grown, each of them told her how important those blessings were to them. Even as young adults now, they still expect a prayer of blessing on special occasions.

In another family, in addition to receiving blessing from the adults, the children lay hands on the adults in blessing. Perhaps such a practice would become particularly symbolic after a child's confirmation or other coming-of-age rite of passage.

On the other hand, asking younger children to bless us can remind us of our need to let them teach us about the sabbath. The Jewish Mishnah says we are to carry no kind of burden on the sabbath. What better way is there to understand this than to identify with the godlike lightness of young children, in their spontaneity, freedom, trust, and playfulness?

Where only adults are present, or where children are present as well, adults may also want to extend the blessing to one another.

The Sabbath Queen

The Talmud says that Rabbi Hanina used to put on his best clothes and say, "Come let us go forth and greet the *Sabbath Queen*." In this spirit of welcome, it is a Jewish custom to read the biblical Song of Songs in praise of the coming of Israel's bride, the sabbath.[9]

During the Friday evening synagogue welcoming service, the congregation "rises and turns to the door to welcome the incoming sabbath," and says:

> Come with rejoicing in song and peace,
> Crown of your people, O Sabbath blessed.
> Toil and labor now shall cease;
> Come Sabbath bride, Sabbath bride of rest.[10]

Queen and *bride* personalize the sabbath. "To name it queen, to call it bride is merely to allude to the fact that its spirit is a reality we meet, rather than an empty span of time we choose to set aside for comfort or recuperation."[11] This reality is not only personal but feminine, imagery woefully rare in active Judeo-Christian sacred symbolism. The sabbath is greeted as a feminine presence, who brings, according to another Jewish tradition, a "second soul" to each person for the duration of the day.

Christians may well consider this poignant practice. It risks some confusion: *Queen* in Christian tradition, if used at all, normally refers to the blessed Virgin Mary, and it is the risen Lord whom Christians most clearly greet. *Bride* normally refers to the church, not to the sabbath. But perhaps the meaning of these terms can be reoriented for Christians. Mary, the "Queen of Heaven" presents the Christ to us. In greeting her at the start of sabbath we greet the one from whose womb Christ is born for us, giving her eternal dignity and first position in the church. The church is the Christian body, born out of the risen Christ.

Thus, in greeting the Sabbath Queen, we greet Mary as vehicle and symbol of all her progeny: the Incarnate Lord, and all who are baptized (visibly or invisibly) in his name. In the Sunday liturgy we will recognize the fullness of this saving mystery. Tonight, on the eve of sabbath, we recognize the bearer of the one through whom, as God's incarnate eternal Word, God's promise of sabbath peace to Israel is offered to all humanity, indeed to all of creation.

For some, this practice of personifying the sabbath may be artificial or of little value. For others, though, it may be one more way of steering the day from an empty span of time toward a personal reality we meet. For many Protestants, especially, it might be one small way of restoring a personal relationship with the feminine sense of the sacred so frequently absent. If at no other time, Mary could at least be greeted in this way during the Christmas season. The whole attitude and practice of sabbath bears out this neglected feminine quality (as culturally defined).

Song of Welcome

One possibility for a brief song is the following, sung to the folk tune of "Michael, Row Your Boat Ashore":

Welcome, welcome, queen of rest, Alleluia!
Guest of joy the Lord has blessed, Alleluia![12]

My daughter especially enjoyed this song when she was young because she could provide an instrumental accompaniment for us on her recorder. Others might use a piano, guitar, or such. No instrumental accompaniment is essential for such a simple song, but it can add to the richness of the occasion and allow instrumental gifts to be offered together with voice. Often we will repeat the song two or three times, since it is so short, or other verses can be composed.

If the Sabbath Queen is not included in your celebration, one alternative song might be a simple chanting of "Peace be unto you," a traditional Jewish welcome of the angels, or this welcome might be expanded to the whole company of heaven, including the communion of saints. This helps to remind us that our celebration is widely shared.

Blessing with Bread and Wine

Using the traditional Jewish blessing with bread and wine again links parents with a proper priestly role, and connects everyone present with Jesus' momentous blessing at the Last Supper, and in the meals of his resurrection appearances, anticipating the church's Sunday liturgy:[13]

The leader of the prayer lifts up the cup of wine (or juice) and prays:

Blessed are you, Lord, God of all creation,
Creator of the fruit of the vine.
Blessed are you, Lord, God of all creation,

> you have taught us the way of holiness through
>   your commandments
> and have granted us your favor
> and given us your holy Sabbath as an inheritance.
> This day is a memorial of creation.
> It is a memorial of the breaking
>   of the bonds of slavery and sin and death.
> Blessed are you, O Lord;
> you make holy the Sabbath day.

The cup is then passed to everyone at the table. When all have taken a drink, the bread is held up and blessed:

> Blessed are you, Lord, God of all creation;
> you bring forth bread from the earth.

The bread is passed and shared, and the meal is served.

The classical Jewish greeting to one another on the sabbath is *shabot shalom*, which means "sabbath peace." Ed Hays suggests such a greeting be said together after the blessing, though he suggests "Happy Sunday" or "Happy Feast" for the wording.[14] The words of the blessing could be revised as you see fit, but I think that these classical Jewish phrases are easily interpretable in Christian terms. They also reinforce a sense of special linkage with the Jewish community, whose divine promise Christians share. This does not obliterate the difference between Christian and Jewish faiths, but it does emphasize the strong overlap, an important connection for children and adults to remember in the face of any temptations toward anti-Semitism.

Such a blessing may be too much for some families as a regular custom. It could have special significance, though, on Passion/Palm Sunday Eve in the anticipation of Jesus' Last Supper, on Holy Thursday, and on those Easter season sabbaths when the scripture lessons speak of the resurrected Jesus making himself known in the breaking of bread.

Eating

Sabbath meals provide opportunity for special celebration of the goodness of creation, and for anticipation of its full transformation in God's own promised time, of which we have been given a foretaste in Jesus Christ. These meals happen in the light of the Sunday eucharistic meal, with its deep memory, its present meeting, its anticipation of the messianic banquet. That central meal potentially turns all meals into agapes—reconciling love feasts—for Christians, but especially the meals that surround it on the sabbath day. Thus the best of what a meal can be should be sought for sabbath meals. Here are a few possibilities for them:

- Grace can be sung or spoken as everyone stands and holds hands. The grace can express special thanks for the opportunity of the sabbath's shalom and ask that we might taste that peace in our home, letting it soften our griefs and trials and bringing beauty to this day.

- A special place can be set that represents everyone else who is meant to share the table with us when God's reign is full: all the saints of earth and the whole company of heaven, from all times and places. Such an empty spot opens the small family circle to its intended eventual fullness. Children and adults alike are reminded of this larger belonging and vocation.

- One or more special guests can be invited to a sabbath meal. This takes a step toward concretizing the larger circle of God's hospitality. The guest might be a relative, friend, institutionalized person, or a foreign student or worker, giving special preference to those who are lonely and poor.

- Another possibility is to place a bulletin board near the table on which you post a liturgical calendar of saints and seasons, and pictures of people not present at your sabbath table. We keep a picture of Juan Ibarra there, a Bolivian boy we support through the Christian Children's Fund. Our support is not much in light of his own and his community's needs, but it vividly reminds us of the vast numbers of materially impoverished and politically oppressed (though quite possibly they are spiritually advanced) people in the world with whom we share God's promise of the kingdom's fullness.

- A small box for money can be kept on the table for everyone's offering: money to be given to some project for the poor that symbolizes the right of everyone in God's grace to share the fruits of the earth with us, and our calling to help foster this just sharing.

Psalms

The Psalms integrate faith, feeling, and experience in Jewish and Christian tradition. They also connect us with all the struggling faithful who have gone before us, whose lips and hearts have shared these same prayer reflections on the experiences of life. The psalms for welcoming the sabbath in Jewish tradition include Psalms 92, 93, and 29; but many others could be used, including the psalm appointed for that evening or for the Sunday liturgy in a lectionary of the church year, or Psalm 126.

Letting a different member of the family select the psalm each week, as well as reading it together in unison or antiphonally, could encourage a sense of shared ownership. Chanting the psalms together in a simple monotone or with slight variations adds an effective and unifying dimension. If so inclined, different members can compose their own simple tonal variations and teach the others.

Saying or chanting the *Gloria Patri* ("Glory Be to the Father") is a classical way of concluding the psalms, bringing them into the full context of the Christian experience of God:

Glory be to the Father [or Creator]
and to the Son [or Redeemer]

and to the Holy Ghost;
as it was in the beginning, is now, and ever shall be,
world without end. Amen. Amen.

If three candles have been lit, this ancient doxology names their lights.

Psalms can be read either at the beginning or the end of the meal, or later in the evening, and/or early on Sunday morning.

In addition to psalms, or an alternative to them, the Gospel lesson for Sunday morning could be read after the meal.

After Dinner

In American culture, Saturday evening (or Sunday, for that matter) is not usually an easy time to stay together as a family or household. Being together for dinner is hard enough, since adults and/or children may be invited out for the evening. One close family with teenage children was told by another parent how amazed she was that they *ever* ate a meal together (much less on Saturday night), since her family was so often scattered at mealtimes, usually eating staggered meals alone if they were home.

My comments have referred primarily to a family with preteen children. Since a sabbath day at this point is not supported by many people, everyone who tries to live it has the dilemma of discerning how far to go in enforcing the sabbath as a special time and resisting pressures from others to turn it into something else. Our family has tried to remain flexible about this on Saturday evening and Sunday afternoons, when we or our children have been invited to be with someone or to go to some event that seems particularly important. We have been inflexible about Sunday mornings, though: no TV, radio, friends (unless they are sharing sabbath observance with us), telephoning (or even answering the telephone). These rules stretch back to Saturday evening by our refusal to allow our children to sleep overnight at someone's house, since it would eat into the heart of the sabbath day on Sunday morning (though we have occasionally allowed them to go to the country with a friend's family for full weekends, and to invite a friend to spend sabbath with us).

Our children have a level of resistance to such rules. We also have found, however, a level of appreciation. Holidays are not simply vacation—literally empty—times, whose anxiety is to be quelled by our latest and escapist wandering impulses. They are meaningful times, wondrous times, gifted times, learned through a particular ritualized framework for time. Life is begun to be sensed as more than an accidental mechanism for our egos to shape out of anxiety; it more easily becomes a gift for us to trust and appreciate.

When we are at home together on Saturday evening, there are other dilemmas: special TV programs and different needs of family members to attend to different things. We want it to be a joyful time for the children and ourselves and not a repressive one, so we have tried to be open to different possibilities. We do try to assure some time during the evening or Sunday when we gather as a family for mutual reflection and play. This may include sharing our experiences during the week with a particular biblical passage each of us chose the previous Sunday (a practice I will describe later); or sharing other experiences of the past week (humorous and otherwise) as well as what we may be looking forward to in our hopes and dreams. Karen Burton Mains suggests a "God hunt" with the family members who are old enough to participate (younger children can be excused to play). This involves reflection on how we may have noticed God's Spirit at work in our lives recently, through such things as answers to prayer, surprising evidence of care, empowerment to do God's work in the world, and any unusual linkage or timing.[15]

Since the sabbath speaks of the mysterious "more" in human life that God symbolizes, parents might consider fun things to do that point to some of the mystery of life, such as magic tricks, kaleidoscopes, telescopes aimed at the sky, wonder stories of the saints, and other stories that leave you in wonder. (These stories may be read or found in special video or television program form.)

We also might sing songs (sacred or secular) that reflect directly or indirectly sabbath peace and promise. Singing, as the Hasidic Rabbi Schlomo Carlbach once pointed out, is something we can do together, as opposed to talking, which can only be done separately. The energy singing raises in us is a freeing, opening, and uniting energy. It is a particularly appropriate activity for the sabbath. If individual members of the family play musical instruments, these can be added. Different members can choose different songs, and shared favorites can be repeated. We have a slowly expanding number of hymns and books of modern musicals that we like to select from. Sometimes dance can be added, such as the simple Shaker circle dance to the tune of "Simple Gifts."[16]

Another possibility for Saturday evening is to incorporate this singing into a brief prayer service, such as the ancient office of compline—the classical, simple bedtime prayers of the church (found in many denominational prayer books or hymnals)—including opportunity for open intercessions and thanksgivings.

Such a service can also incorporate a brief rite of reconciliation: Each person in silence can reflect on ways he or she has offended others that week, especially others in the family, and ask for one another's and God's forgiveness, ending with a corporate confession and a scriptural declaration of God's willingness to forgive those who repent. Such a brief mutual rite can help to cleanse the family of accumulated pollutions and free it for a fresh start, together and separately. The earlier on the sabbath (or even before) it begins, the better for such cleansing.

Another kind of cleansing involves water. The practice of remembering thankfully the power and symbolism of water in God's hands is not new. For Orthodox Jews bathing is one more of countless human activities during which an ancient special blessing is said. The *mikvah* ritual bath is taken before sundown as part of the preparation for sabbath. For Christians there is the added importance of the renewing water of baptism, extended in Celtic and other historical Christian practice to holy wells for healing and blessing.

The fast-paced, denatured consciousness of a majority of people in the industrialized world leads to a dulled, fragmented consciousness that usually zips through a bath with no appreciation or connection with the fuller world with which it relates us. A bath is just one more taken-for-granted routine whose waters, for all we are aware, are one more human mechanical invention (an attitude about water brought to an extreme when someone asked a park ranger at Yellowstone, "What time do they turn on the geyser?"). One antidote to this menacingly dulled consciousness is a purposeful intention to connect something as ordinary as a bath with its wondrous and extraordinary meanings and uses in sacred history. Such an attitude is enhanced by the physically relaxed, surrendering, open state of mind that a shower or bath can allow. One minister I know says that her bath is her greatest "alone prayer time," with a closed door where she cannot be interrupted, and a relaxed state where many people encountered in her day naturally float to mind, people she lightly "offers up" in prayer.

At the end of the evening children can be put to bed with a special prayer that gives thanks for the sabbath peace of the Lord. In the order for compline previously mentioned, there is a special prayer for Saturday night:

> We give you thanks, O God, for revealing your son, Jesus Christ, to us by the light of his resurrection! Grant that as we sing your glory at the close of this day, our joy may abound in the morning as we celebrate the Paschal Mystery; through Jesus Christ our Lord.

On Saturday evening we begin our move toward this celebration. Whatever we do that evening, it is a good guideline deliberately to slow down our normal physical and mental pace. Sometimes we may need a little simple yoga or slow deep breathing to help this happen, especially if we are emerging from a particularly hectic day or week.

We can begin to let spaces appear between our actions. We can let an attitude of "sufficiency for now" emerge; we need nothing more than what is presented. Our striving loosens. The time emerges as a gift, as graced, in which we are invited simply to trust, to be held in the arms of the Eternally Near One, visible to us in the arms of Mary, the Sabbath Queen, who bears the Christ to us in whose cosmic body we live. When we fall asleep Saturday night, we might utter Jesus' prayer, "Into your hands I commit my spirit," and let ourselves sleep trusting that we are upheld before, through, and beyond all of our works—the trust that is sabbath peace.

Sunday Morning

We can awake in the morning faintly aware of that trace of early Sunday quiet still present in most neighborhoods. Our first words can be a silent prayer of thanksgiving for the continuance of the sabbath day, and perhaps we might read the joyful Psalm 100. If we are beginning the sabbath now, then all or part of the welcoming service described for Saturday evening can take place around breakfast.

Silence

After a special breakfast, our house falls into silence for an hour. Each family member goes to his/her room or to some other place alone. It is the only waking hour in the week when the house is silent. You can feel the stillness opening and inviting a reflective mind sensitive to the hidden Spirit among us.

The primary guideline for the hour is that we be present to life as a gift from God. For very young children such an hour is not likely to be possible. Older ones, though, are capable of such quiet activities as reading, writing, or drawing for an hour. We encourage them just to let something spontaneous flow through them if they write or draw, and to be thankfully aware of God's love for them and for the way that love comes through everything around them that they see and enjoy, even sometimes through what is painful. Occasionally our children like to spend part of the time staring at the wonders of the underwater world in their fish tanks.

Children need aids for this time. As my wife has told me, "It is hard to be good without something to be good with." She once read our children an English novel that made reference to a special box of aids for a family of children during Sunday quiet time. That led us, when the children were young, to make a "sabbath box" for each of them, brought out only on Sundays, containing things like watercolors, sketch pads, and new books. The children often spontaneously create things they enjoy making and give them to us or to each other, or otherwise share their experiences at the end of quiet time.

Lest I overidealize what children might do in this time, you should know that sometimes our son feels that reviewing of his football cards is adequate recognition of the sabbath, or our daughter feels that painting her face in imitation of the latest fashion magazine model is sufficient. Who knows, in God's mysterious generosity, how these might be murky avenues of sabbath appreciation too (though the thought of such a possibility might require a particularly generous mind!).

For up to an hour, children usually are able to appreciate the difference of this time. More than an hour, I think, would become repressive for them. Time and experiment are needed to sort out just what is appropriate, but the effort can be instructive for everyone.

Adults can spend such time in spiritual reading, meditation and prayer, or writing and drawing of their own: those ways of being present to which we would not likely get around if explicit time was not set apart for them.

There is historical precedence for this silence. In early Puritan households, for example, families kept periods of silence in preparation for Sunday worship.[1]

Scripture

At the end (or beginning) of this period each child can be responsible for reading aloud all or part of one of the scripture lessons assigned for that Sunday in the lectionary, followed by a brief discussion of its meaning. Each of us chooses one phrase from the lessons as our special phrase for the week, something that really caught our attention—that we take with us through the week. Sometimes the phrase is chosen later from the collect for the day or other words of the Sunday liturgy. The phrases can be written out on slips of paper and hung on the family bulletin board or in our rooms. This is a simple adaptation of the classical monastic practice of *lectio divina*, wherein we stop reading scripture and focus on a particular word or phrase that attracts us strongly, somehow pregnant with a particular truth that needs to be birthed in us at this time.

Such attention to scripture before liturgy can be a chore for children at first (and sometimes for adults). But it can help them to be involved in the liturgy and its lessons and sermons more attentively and with more understanding. The practice of reading scripture and prayer with an open mind, listening for a particular gifted phrase, connects them with a profound historic discipline of attentiveness that we hope becomes a lifetime habit. If such attentiveness is well cultivated, it will spill over into a way of listening more sensitively to everything they read and hear in life, sensitive to the gifts of little revelations that are meant for us. Such listening involves a very different motive from our dominant commercial and technical listening, where titillation or control, rather than revelation, reign supreme.

Liturgy

If the family attends an early church service, an hour of silence may be more practical on Saturday evening or Sunday afternoon. This raises the question of the right time for gathering with the larger church for *sabbath worship*. The answer, first of all, is that there is no single right time for everyone. That is why services, according to denomination and local church, vary from Saturday evening through Sunday evening, with Roman Catholics often providing a choice of times throughout the twenty-four hours.

With small congregations there often isn't any choice—11:00 A.M. (or whatever time) *is* the service. This has the symbolic value of gathering a whole local fellowship of the church at one time, where they can see, pray, and interact with each other. Mutual belonging and accountability can be reinforced and affirmed in such a situation. In an ever-increasing number of churches, though, gathering at the same time is prevented by the large numbers of people in the congregation, or by the varying schedules of people in our complex society. In any case, I would like to suggest a sabbath criterion for evaluating the time of church gathering: whatever will best allow the service to be a jewel set off by its spacious sabbath bed, rather than one smothered in a field of wind-blown straw.

Corporate worship can be the pinnacle of the Christian sabbath, but it is not the sabbath. It is unrealistic to expect people to be fully present in liturgy when it is surrounded by rushed, distracting activities of every kind. A dulled or distracted mind cannot worship with any depth. Preachers and worship leaders sense this, but rather than focusing on people's sabbath time surrounding the service, they instead sometimes might try ever more desperately to force people's attention during the service through dramatic or frivolously humorous sermons, and through exciting music or other elements that can easily cross the line from worship to consumer entertainment.

Such efforts are bound to fail spiritually in the end, I think, because they cannot do for the people what the people must do for themselves. It is our own prayer, reading, silence, rest, and appreciative presence to this giftedness of life in Christ that we feed into corporate worship. This is the spacious bed that sets off liturgy and lets it radiate among us. No great dramatic liturgy or sermon is needed to force-feed the gospel into people's scattered minds. A proper sabbath setting brings its own attunement to the Word and sacrament. The slightest, simplest sound, word, or sight can then set off a holy resonance within and among us. This is why the simplest liturgy is often experienced so fully in the midst of a retreat, when we have ordered sabbath time together.

Sometimes even when we are scattered, we still can taste this quality vicariously, through others whose sabbath is full. That is why worship leaders, those who are most visible in liturgies, especially need sabbath preparation for liturgy, lest they enter rushed and distracted, thereby diverting from the quality of presence that the congregation needs from them. Such preparation is difficult with all the demands placed on such leaders, but it is not impossible. The last few minutes before entering the sanctuary can most fruitfully be spent in silence, stillness, and prayer, letting one's own ego-fears and plans recede in the face of the awesome, intimate, sustaining Presence in our midst.

If we find ourselves in a situation where there is no church that we can attend on Sundays, either because of physical location, or the nature of the local church, or our own physical condition, then we still need to pray with and for the larger church and world at home or wherever we are. Such intercession is not optional. The Lord's Day is not a private time. It is the most corporate time of the week, even if we are completely alone physically. It is the least appropriate time for us to dwell on our differences, self-pity, and narrow concerns. It is a day of unity amidst our diversity and of intercession for all, that we will be led to the full, just unity of God's shalom.[2] Intercessory prayer lifts us above the temptations of self-focus and isolation. It leads us toward that overflow of concern that enlivens the work of ministry. Such prayer for others is the minimal way of fulfilling that ancient dimension of the true sabbath day: "works of mercy," for such prayer indeed is the foundational mercy work of Christians.

Increasingly we find small informal groups of Christians meeting together on Sundays and other days for prayer, reflection, fellowship, and sometimes Eucharist, often reflecting the early church's simplicity and fervor. Out of such groups great religious communities have been born in the past, sometimes remaining in communion with the larger church, sometimes (especially after the Reformation) splitting off into separate Christian bodies.

For many people liturgy and fellowship come alive the most in such settings. Such groups are a standing challenge to the church's dangers of overinstitutionalized formalism, and a historical base of renewal. They can provide a depth of identity and accountability that sometimes frees their members to live lives of clear and steady witness and strength in the world.

On the negative side, they can become fanatical, self-righteous, and narrow, losing the fullness of the church. These temptations diminish when the group values the stimulus and heterogeneity of the larger church and continues to worship with it. Indeed local churches sometimes take the initiative in forming such subgroups, but I think more often they arise spontaneously among those desiring a more intense or differently weighted spiritual life than the formal congregation fosters.

As the church continues to attempt a viable adaptation to the complex and diverse life patterns and spiritual hungers of our evolving society, it might well be that such small subcommunities will need to receive increasing support from the church in many situations, despite their possible threat to controlled, centralized, and familiar patterns of the local church. Members of such groups could be vital support for one another's rhythm of sabbath and ministry.

In northern Sweden this basic way has become institutionalized, with people meeting in small groups for worship and study, gathering as a larger community of faith on six *church days* during the year. With small congregations this practice may allow far better stewardship. Many costly large buildings would not have to be maintained. More time might be available for sabbath rest, prayer, and ministry in the world, as time-consuming institutional maintenance was reduced. Perhaps fewer full-time clergy would have to be supported, or their deployment could be scattered through a number of extended-family cell groups. Such groups could be weekly base communities, with larger gatherings in cathedral-style churches on special occasions, especially high holy days of the liturgical year.[3]

Sunday Afternoon and Closure

$\mathcal{T}$he afternoon can be the hardest time to attend to sabbath for many people.[1] We may well feel a certain sluggishness or restlessness, a touch of the high-noon fever of ancient monastic awareness called *acedia*. If we have just completed a Sunday liturgy, we might feel a certain sense of anticlimax. No doubt this is a major psychological reason for the historical practice of ending the sabbath as a special time at noon in much of Christian Europe.

On the other hand, if the liturgy was particularly graced for us, then we may well feel an overflow into the afternoon. Life and community take on renewed appreciation in our inner spiritual eye. We are moved to continue the liturgy in our hearts, in joy and desire to share its fruits. This may take the form of an especially appreciated simple Sunday dinner, with special prayer, table, and candles. A friend or stranger from church or elsewhere might well be invited to share this meal with us, affirming the hospitality that flows from the liturgy. In a few churches it is a time when the ancient sabbath agape meal is shared in the church with the poor of the community. My own parish focuses on the senior citizens of the neighborhood at this time.

Another classic way of carrying over the liturgy into works of mercy in the afternoon may take the form of visiting a homebound person or going to a nursing home, prison, or hospital. The sabbath helps slow us down to the speed of those who are in such an enforced rest, freeing us for more patience and relaxed sharing together. In such meetings we become philanthropists with time, not just money and other possessions.[2] Fellowship with one's own relatives and friends also is traditional at this time. With the ever loosening and fragmenting bonds of family and communal relationships today, the old practice of *Sunday visitin'* is not to be scorned. It helps maintain and build the social fabric of the larger community, which an inclusive sabbath peace encourages. The givenness of our relationships with family and some friends also reflects the sabbath as a given, ascribed quality of time, not an earned, achieved one. An acquaintance told me of a comprehensive way that she and the other sixteen members of her extended family have been keeping sabbath together for ten years: they gather on Sundays and go to church, eat a meal together, tell stories, sing, and dance; it's a shared and joyful time that has been very meaningful to them.

Sports are not to be scorned at this time if they express for us the incarnate joy of physical gifts, movement, and imagination (as opposed to a calculated, complex competitiveness bent on winning at all costs). At times simple sports like jogging or tennis can be a way of meditation: giving our bodies something repetitive to do has a way of settling and even stilling our minds, allowing deeper participation in gifted-life-as-it-is. If we have children participating in a Sunday afternoon team sport, we can sit and watch them with that appreciative ease of someone whose main responsibility is to just enjoy what's happening.

Sunday afternoon can be a good time for a personal or family-friends walk or hike in the woods, at the seashore, or in the hills (depending on where we live), or for just sitting in the yard or park, perhaps best done in silence. Sabbath is a time for touching God's creation more closely, feeling the wind, sun, or rain on our face, and taking time to appreciate the living beings of nature. It is not a time when we must do something to nature; rather, it is a time simply to be present in nature, letting everything lead us to wonder rather than to manipulation.

This is the attitude of contemplation, which is both a symbol and a practice of sabbath: " It enjoys rather than uses, it rests rather than acts."[3] Lightness marks such time: light ego, light humor, light action, so that there is room for the light to be known more intimately.[4]

For others the afternoon may be a time for reading or one of the arts, whatever might aid our simple presence in life as free and gifted from God's hand. If such activity is *work* for us, it is likely to pull us away into the drivenness of the week. If it is essentially *play*, then we are closer to God's sheer joy in creating us and all else.

Even our dialogue together can soar beyond the workaday world's constraints. We can dream together of how life might be at its fullest, letting our imagination and biblical promises take us wherever they might lead. One family I know makes it a rule on this day that no one can criticize another. It is a day of acceptance and not judgment. They report that other children (teenagers) tend to drop by their house on Sunday afternoons, as though they sensed the soothing difference of such a mutually accepting atmosphere.

It is worth noting the intimacy of acceptance, play, and wonder with *laughter* in these activities. Humor was a sadly missing quality in the Puritan sabbath. Humor, as any emotional response, can be distorted and distracting. But it also can be a little transcendent sign of shalom.

Closure

However we spend the afternoon, its drawing to a close marks the end of the sabbath day. This closure needs special recognition, just as the sabbath's beginning does.

The Jewish community historically has developed a special ritual for ending sabbath after sundown, a rite called *havdalah*, "separation," which divides the sabbath from other days. It includes the
lighting of a double-wicked, intertwined candle, symbolizing our
sabbath-revealed communion with God, blessing prayers, the
passing of a container of sweet spices for everyone symbolically to
smell the sweetness of sabbath and take it into the week, farewell
songs to the sabbath, and quenching of the candle in a glass of wine
(or some other sweet liquid). The candle, once lit, traditionally is
given to the youngest person present to hold.

My family has developed a closing ritual of its own that overlaps with this traditional ending, which is shared with others who
happen to be with us at the time. We begin a special supper, a kind
of high tea that includes all kinds of good things to eat. We bring
this food into the living room, the only time we eat there during the
week. Candles are lit. A blessing is said. During the meal we talk
informally about the day and sometimes about the coming week.
About halfway through, one of us reads aloud to the others for
about fifteen minutes. Currently we are reading a wondrous yet
very human story about a family and its adventures. We read seri-
ally, week by week, until the story is finished, and we read it at no
other time. The story provides an ongoing drama, a window,
through which we subtly see, share, and enjoy the way life can un-
fold in God's hidden grace and human response. It has a way of en-
larging our common experience and, as well, our reference points
as a family. We refer back to incidents in the story during the week
as related things happen to us.

After the last bite of dessert is devoured, satisfied with this sen-
sate sign of the yearned-for heavenly banquet, we say or sing a
psalm or canticle together, give thanks for the personal presence of
sabbath with us, pray for God's full shalom to come on earth, and
for the ways our lives can be graced to assist and share that coming during the week.

Then we continue with the Jewish custom of passing a jar or box of spices around for everyone to smell, a reminder of the sweet savor of the sabbath to take into the week. Gabe Huck suggests that the spices be held up while praying:

> Our God, we thank you for the joy and rest of this day.
> As we inhale the fragrance of the spices,
> We pray that the days ahead
>   may bring sweetness to our lives
>   and to the lives of all your children.
> May we yearn for the coming of your reign,
>   the sabbath without end.
> Blessed are you, Lord God of all creation,
>   Creator of the spices.[5]

Finally we extinguish the candles with a prayer of thanksgiving for the fire of God's Spirit, which cannot be quenched.

The Sabbath and Other Days

In Jewish tradition all the following days of the week are numbered in relation to the sabbath. The first three days belong to the previous sabbath, the next three to the coming sabbath, so it "casts its radiance before and behind."[6] Heschel elaborates this poignantly:

> The sabbath cannot survive in exile, a lonely stranger among days of profanity. . . . All days of the week must be spiritually consistent with the Day of Days. All our life should be a pilgrimage to the seventh day. Sabbath is the counterpoint of living, the melody sustained throughout all agitations and vicissitudes which menace our conscience; our awareness of God's presence in the world.[7]

For most Christians, this day is the first day of the week, Sunday, which irradiates all others.

The biblical scholar and Swedish Lutheran Bishop Krister Stendahl once said, "I find it important to reflect on 'the Christian week,' that delightfully immoral structure that begins with a 'day off.' I find that arrangement beautiful and full of meaning. We do not work a long week in order to get to the Sabbath. We begin in the sign and mood and celebration of the new creation, the Resurrection."[8]

Personal Adaptation

I have described for you one set of ways for living through a Christian sabbath day. Endless variations are possible, given our circumstances and the ways we are called to structure this time. Always, though, the sabbath day will include two dimensions: first, a *negative* one of a different space, set aside from the usual demands of the human producer. This freed-up space then allows and needs a *positive* dimension, wherein the space is filled with the personal presence of the Sabbath Queen and Lord, and all they bring of authentic rest, joy, connectedness, and intimacy.

The negative dimension brings the pain of relinquishing our works. The positive dimension brings the fruits of this surrender. Together these dimensions embody the rhythm of the Paschal Mystery at the heart of Christian sabbath and Christian life, dying and rising with Christ, letting go and embracing the grace that is revealed.

For those just beginning such an extended practice, as I noted earlier, it might be best to begin slowly, with just a few hours at first, and then gradually extend and experiment with the time in the light of your situation, until a right pattern is established. If you live with your family, you may wish only to assure that you do at least one thing together that is different and spacious on Sundays. Many of the ingredients I have proposed can be moved to different parts of the day depending on your situation. Also, many other possibilities than these may occur to you. There may be times when you are called to live through sabbath time with no preplanned structure at all, just with your simple intent to "hang out" with God, letting Christ's Spirit guide your sabbath dance steps moment by moment.

Don't be discouraged too quickly by interruptions, lack of consistent motivation, or competing desires. Give the day a chance to grow in value. Above all, find someone else to support, and ideally to join you in this discipline, lest you give up out of sheer aloneness in it as an individual or household. In most Christian settings it will take a long time to reclaim as a corporate practice. The beachhead for its renewal at this point, I think, must lie with a scattering of mutually supportive people.

Those people whose work involves a kind of open-time job description (as opposed to one with set hours) especially need support if they are to avoid the temptation *not* to shift gears on Sundays and instead turn it into just one more work day. My own job description involves such openness. Intentional sabbath time has come to me as an enormous relief from the compulsive pressure to keep working whenever there is space for it.

Yet it takes time and help to move through the stages of (1) continual work with a twinge of guilt; (2) not working, but guilty and uncomfortable about this too; to (3) truly accepting sabbath as a mandated gift and part of one's vocation.

If sabbath time slips into an oppressive burden, or a law through which we feel we will be saved, then our attitude needs cleansing. If this cleansing is not forthcoming, then perhaps the practice should be dropped until our attitude is liberated. Sabbath time is meant to be opportunity, not burden—a window that reveals grace, not grace itself.

Earlier I recognized the reality that for a number of working people Sunday cannot be a sabbath day, but that it can be practiced, at least partially, on whatever day off one has. I would like to extend this group to include parish clergy. Psychologically, and usually practically, Sunday is the central work day for them. Most clergy badly need a different day of the week, or at least part of a day, during which they can experience more extensive sabbath rest than is usually possible on their Sundays.

I don't mean by this merely having time for private groggy entertainment, alternative work, or escape. I mean real sabbath time, wherein one lets oneself simply *be* in prayer, jogging, reading, or other activity, with nothing whatsoever to produce, to make happen, to plan—even for oneself. Such times can help condition usually hard-driving and driven clergy to slow down and let their hearts sink effortlessly deeper into the gospel they carry in their labors: the gospel proclaiming that God reveals an astoundingly free guiding love for us in Christ, through the Spirit, a love dependent on none of our works, asking only our trust and our attentiveness. We can afford to rest in such a divine Lover, whose living waters will refresh us if we still our crowded busyness for a while.

Pastoral leadership on Sundays can help to open up and protect such receptive, spacious time for others, especially during the liturgy. Clergy at least partially sacrifice their own sabbath time in order to provide it for others. They in turn need their own receptive sabbath at a time when they are not responsibly in charge.

With persons who do not gainfully work, either voluntarily (as in retirement) or involuntarily (when out of a job), sabbath time can take on a different quality. The rhythm of steady work and rest is absent in their lives, but routine and volunteer work at home and elsewhere is usually maintained, and this can cease. Sabbath time can be gifted for such people just as for others.

The unemployed person can approach the sabbath as a time of renewed hope, countering the temptation to collapse into depression or bitterness. The retired person also can allow the sabbath to be a time of encouragement, offering God's promise of meaning and worth through the pain of physical decline and other changes. For very old people and for the dying, sabbath is a reminder of the one who is faithful through the rest and cleansing of death—and beyond.

PART V

Living Other Sabbath Times

Times of Passage

$\mathcal{M}$any times I have distinguished between the sabbath as a weekly special *day* and as a special *time*, which can be part of any day. Already I have dealt briefly with the value of setting aside at least a few minutes daily for a minisabbath, a time of just being: in prayer, scripture, stretching exercises, jogging, or whatever is right for us. Such time can be stretched into longer periods of retreat or pilgrimage.[1] It also can come during those enforced waiting periods of the week: waiting in lines, for transportation, for someone to come, for sleep. Sleep itself can be seen as a daily enforced sabbath, a receptive, sometimes revealing, passage between one active day and the next, during which time "the soul is enfolded in One."[2]

From the many possibilities for sabbath time, I have selected one example for particular attention—times of passage.

An essential part of human living is moving through special times of passage: from one life stage to another, singlehood to marriage or vowed religious community, childlessness to parental responsibility; between wellness and sickness, private life and public office, work and vacation or unemployment; moving from one job to the next, from agnosticism to committed faith, from life to death.

The church historically surrounds many of these times with special rites: baptism, confirmation, ordination, commissioning, blessing of marriages, Communion, laying on of hands, anointing, and burial.[3] Each of these passages takes us another step further in life; each has its own dread, joy, and challenge; and each tests our trust and understanding of God and invites us more deeply into God's presence.

This invitation normally can be heard and best responded to if we allow intentional sabbath time to be part of the passage. It means taking anywhere from a day to a month or longer where we spend our primary time simply being present to God in prayer and rest. If possible, at least part of this time should be spent in a place away from normal pressures and routines, a place that invites calm reflection, such as a retreat center. Both scripture and church history witness to the value of such intentional periods of withdrawal.

This time normally includes some kind of self-examination, where we look for the hidden footsteps of God in our lives, and how we have responded to them. It may well lead to confession, before God alone or, if it is our custom, before another person, asking for assurance of God's pardon, healing, and cleansing from the past, and strength for a new beginning.

Such time would be marked especially by an intent to surrender our lives and this new step in trust to the Lord, and to realize God's will for us in this development. The intent can be enhanced by the reading of scripture, by simple open prayer and meditation, and by meeting with a spiritual friend, to whom we bare our soul and ask for prayer and reflection with us on the step we are taking.

A major passage I would like to single out for illustration here is the one from adolescence to adulthood. It needs special mention because it is so neglected and protracted in our culture.

Practically speaking, this passage comes in bits and pieces through such events as sexual maturation, obtaining a first driver's license, church confirmation, high school or college graduation, a first job, and leaving home. Our commercial and individualistic culture tends to encourage adolescents not to become full adults, despite these various opportunities. Life often is publicly portrayed as a narcissistic advance from one ego-possession to the next, with only expedient reference to responsibility and corporate vision. It is not easy to make the passage from a cared-for and narrowly self-centered youth to an adult steward of human and environmental life, responsible for his or her care and development.

In light of this necessity, I believe the church can be particularly helpful by setting the stage for full adulthood far more seriously than it usually does in confirmation, or whatever else it calls its sacralizing rite of passage to adulthood. The ingredient I would press for is a serious guided withdrawal into a quality of sabbath time for an extended period, perhaps as short as a weekend or as long as a month or more. This might best be done in the late teens, when a person perhaps is ready for an early adult faith.[4]

Preparation for adult initiation into the early church included prayer, fasting, study, and testing of "the manner of life and the moral firmness of the candidate."[5] The preparation could extend as long as three years; the initiation practices overlapped those of other religious groups at the time, and modern anthropological studies show us how frequent these elements are in adult initiations of many cultures.[6]

There are a great variety of ways that a special quality of sabbath time could mark this preparation, depending on individual, group, and church circumstances. My suggestions would include choosing Lent as the season of the church year that will best support this preparation. A number of churches today make a special point of tying baptism-confirmation back into its early church Easter context. That season provides some sense of the larger church, past and present, sharing a dimension of preparation with the initiates.

Several spiritually mature adults who have rapport with teenagers, including a priest/minister, could take the teenagers desiring adult baptism/confirmation for the week of spring vacation (if this timing is consonant among their schools). If this is not possible, then they could be taken away for a retreat weekend both at the beginning and end of Lent. In either case, meetings together would surround these retreat times, both preparing for them and following them up.

The retreat itself would be marked by a radically different quality of time than teenagers usually experience. It could include blocks of solitary and corporate silence, with preparation in how to live through these times in meditation and prayer. Fasting or at least abstinence (for example, from animal flesh and desserts) could mark the entire time if it was a weekend (except perhaps for a final festive meal).

Group reflection, with scripture, church history, and contemporary social perspectives offered as background, could be scheduled at particular times to consider what participants would be giving up and taking on as adult Christians. This would include reflection on their personal prayer, study, moral standards, stewardship of body and money, and sense of vocation, as well as in their corporate life and concerns for the justice, peace, and creativity of the larger community. They also could consider how they can support one another in carrying out an adult way of life, in the framework of a culture and peers that in many ways will not support them, but instead offer competing ways and understandings of life. Perhaps a personal written covenant statement that includes one's own sense of what is important in Christian adulthood related to one's gifts and limitations would help to climax such reflection. This could be tested with others for realism and inclusiveness. It might include commitment to an annual review, in the light of one's continuing unfolding.

The alternative ways that dominate our cafeteria culture can make it very difficult for people to give themselves wholeheartedly and steadily in trust to any particular way, unless they do so in a very rigid and sectarian fashion. Young people (and old ones too) desperately need support for a middle way, such as I am suggesting here, that lies between sectarianism on the one hand, and an overvulnerability to the culture on the other: "tossed to and fro and blown about by every wind of doctrine, by people's trickery, by their craftiness in deceitful scheming" (Eph. 4:14).

The retreat also could include periods of corporate prayer and singing, and simple stretching and breathing exercises to help relax yet energize their often very tense bodies.

Scheduled private interviews with one of the adult leaders could also be an important ingredient. An interview could concentrate on the person's sense of difficulty and readiness for adult Christian responsibility, on what kinds of focus his or her continuing preparation needs to have, perhaps on a tailor-made rule of life (including daily times and methods of prayer) to carry out not only during the balance of the preparatory period, but afterward as well. If a personal statement has been written, as suggested above, it might be brought into the meeting for review.

The person also could be encouraged to select some adult as a spiritual mentor with whom he or she could meet periodically (perhaps monthly) for review of the rule and of his or her spiritual life in general. In traditions where the rite of reconciliation is offered formally, this also might be a time for confession and absolution, a clearing of the decks before the new adult life stage. In other traditions this might be done in silence together, or in self-selected pairs, followed by a corporate confession and absolution.

Such a retreat over a week, or divided into two weekends surrounding the preparatory period, could provide a significant and unforgettable dimension of a serious rite of passage. Not only could it better condition participants for adult responsibility in the church and world, but it could also provide an exposure to extended sabbath time that would set a pattern for the rhythm of their lives. A daily, a weekly, and a more extensive annual period of sabbath time could emerge from this experience as a highly valued framework for living a full Christian adult rhythm of life.

Teenagers, of course, do not mature evenly. Their readiness for adult initiation needs to be a joint decision by them and some responsible adult in the church or home. At the same time, having a particular late-teenage time set for this rite of passage gives them opportunity to anticipate that, indeed, it is time for them to take on fresh adult Christian responsibility and privilege in the world. Their parents need to be brought into this process carefully, if they are to be counted on for the support the teenagers need.

One reason, I think, that the *Star Wars* films have been so immensely popular over the years is the identification of youth with Luke Skywalker, the young hero. We see him move through a passage from a kind of domestic child identification and narrow vision to a responsible adult. He struggles with and through this transition with the aid of an adult guru. The passage includes a quality of sabbath time preparation (brought out especially in the second film): a withdrawn, seriously tested strengthening period, cut short by discernment. Princess Leia's adultlike responsible behavior and status reinforces this sense of emergence.

Youth (and many adults as well) are starved for adequate means of passage and adult mentors today—processes and people that can help draw out of them their full calling and capacity. Jesus, in being such a person for his disciples, promised that they in faith would do greater works than he, thus envisioning their fullest potential in God. Opportunities for youth to be guided through a serious passage toward adulthood are a major responsibility and opportunity for the church. A quality of sabbath time is an essential dimension of this process.

A special note needs to be made about the relationship of such a rite of passage to the emerging "men's movement," as well as the revolutionary movements of women in recent decades. The new men's movement has lamented the enormous price that men, women, and the whole culture pay for the lack of adequate initiation into mature manhood. They attribute much individual, social, and national (war) violence to such things as men's conditioned fear of losing control, fear of vulnerability, and out-of-touchness with compassion and real feelings. The mature man is one who can integrate qualities such as compassion and vulnerability with responsible firmness and focused strength. Put into a spiritual context, they sound very much like what Christ asked of his disciples and of himself. The same could be said of many qualities espoused by women's movements.

It could be very helpful to have men meet separately for part of their initiation to consider qualities of adult Christian manhood, and women to meet separately to consider qualities of adult Christian womanhood that responsibly accepts, for example, new power and interdependence (rather than dependency) in social relationships as these are called for, as modeled by great spiritual women. For both genders, these qualities would need to be seen in the positive light of the unique personalities involved. Then both groups could join and, beyond sharing their struggles and images, seek their huge overlaps in Christ, "in whom there is neither male nor female."

Two other passages need special mention: sickness and dying. These are especially difficult for full sabbathing, if our minds are feverished and fogged. They become enforced sabbaths, where we have no choice but to lie back and be. Our prayer will be simple in such times. We usually do not have energy for anything straining or complex. But our prayer is most important in these passages.

Sickness sometimes comes as a signal that we have not allowed sufficient voluntary sabbath time in our lives. We have stretched the bow of the apostle John's story in strain and striving until it breaks. If this is so, then sickness comes as a gift, an opportunity, to pass from a works-righteous, controlling way of life to one that allows more trust in God's working, and more structured times of sabbath where this can be reinforced and appreciated. Our central sabbath prayer in such sickness can be for simple surrender to God's grace, and for fresh opportunity to live in the light of that grace.

Death comes as the last human passage, the one that requires the most trust, for we cannot know what lies beyond. If our minds are clear enough, and we sense impending death, then surrender is asked of us most completely. If our sabbath times in life have prepared us for this surrendering, it will come a bit more naturally now, but I think almost always with struggle and grieving before the peace. We pray the last time for release in Christ from the bonds our sin and ignorance have woven in this life, and pray for the world's release as well, as a priestly intercessor of the body (lay or ordained). We give thanks for the grace of this life. Finally, we offer ourselves to the eternal sabbath of God, in blind trust: "Into your hand I commit my spirit" (Ps. 31:5; see also Luke 23:46; Acts 7:59). We rest in God, most literally and helplessly.[7]

The opportunity for other sabbath times in our lives needs to be seen in the light of the opportunities for leisure time in Western nations that are increasing proportionately to the development of a technologically advanced, labor-reduced economy. As we have seen historically, human beings do not usually find it easy to live through such discretionary periods of time. We are tempted to turn them into work or dulled escape. The church has a special opportunity and responsibility to help people reflect on how such time can be fruitfully spent, in the light of its historic rhythm of sabbath and ministry. This chapter is meant to be a small stimulus to that reflection process. Much more reflection needs to be done related to the great variety of situations in which leisure time is available, voluntarily or involuntarily.[8]

The Rest and Labor of Love

$\mathcal{L}$ove labors and rests in its beloved. "[1]

Love in the triune God is open, connecting, freeing, playful, painful, transforming. Its two faces are labor and rest, ministry and sabbath. Such love is the fulfillment of all the commandments. For this we are born. Yet this love does not come easily. We are an open Dr. Jekyll who lives with a Mr. Hyde ever lurking to twist the freedom of that love into a closed, calculating fist of evil, delusion, and separation. We live internally divided in this way. Our social situations mirror this personal split. Our life in Christ is a struggle and a plea to reconcile in God the split-off beast within and without and let its energies be transformed by the river of grace that flows through all that is.

Our bodies reflect this struggle too. Their healing, cleansing, enlivening energy channels become blocked in places, and clenching pain, disease, and distortion follow. There is so much in and around us that drives them closed. Thus we must return again and again to various treatments for their opening. Our love in Christ is like this. We yearn for a new and stabilized level of its flow through and around us, yet we find it blocked again and again. Our spiritual practices, underlain by gifted faith and desire for God's fullness, are the treatments with which we are endowed to open us to

Love's flow again and again.

A rhythm of sabbath and ministry time is a foundational discipline, a framework for all our disciplines. It is a rhythm that God provides to human life for its care, cleansing, and opening to grace. This rhythm is not for one day or one week or one year only. It is for life. Broken human beings cannot expect God's wise love to hold in our awareness once and for all. The rhythm, as a permanent discipline, symbolizes this reality. We can pray that over the years it will help us appreciate Holy Love's desire to touch those cramped places of dammed-up spiritual energy in our lives and release us for ever deeper, wiser, steadier, and bolder praise and ministry.

Sabbath and ministry are united by a single-hearted desire for this knowing love to live through us, in all that we are and do, and indeed to live through all creation. In graced time, this rest and labor of love mingle with ever greater intimacy, and a sabbath heart lives in us through all our labors.

> In one single moment and at the same time, love labors and rests in its beloved. And the one is strengthened by the other: for the loftier the love, the greater is the rest, and the greater is the rest, the closer is the love; for the one lives in the other.[2]

> [Jesus said] "Come to me, all you that are weary and are carrying heavy burdens, and I will give you rest. Take my yoke upon you, and learn from me. . . . For my yoke is easy, and my burden is light."
>
> Matthew 11:28-30

> My times are in your hand.
> Psalm 31:15

$\mathcal{N}$otes

Chapter 1: An Alternative Way

1. Classical Christian discernment of spirits involves the gifted discernment of the origin of forces moving in and among us: whether they be primarily of God, ego, or the demonic.

2. Winton U. Solberg, *Redeem the Time: The Puritan Sabbath in Early America* (Cambridge, Mass.: Harvard University Press, 1977), ix.

3. Ibid., 301.

4. This scientific support for the importance of our subject was summarized in detail in the third chapter of my book *Spiritual Friend* (New York: Paulist Press, 1980). See especially Victor W. Turner, *The Ritual Process: Structure and Anti-Structure* (Chicago, Ill.: Aldine Publishing Co., 1969), and Bruce D. Reed, *The Dynamics of Religion: Process and Movement in Christian Churches* (London: Darton, Longman and Todd, 1978).

5. The Jewish community, of course, also shares this task on a smaller scale.

Chapter 2: Hebrew Scripture

1. Mircea Eliade, *The Sacred and the Profane* (New York: Harper & Row, 1957), 93–111.

2. See Dayan I. Grunfeld, *The Sabbath: A Guide to Its Understanding and Observance* (Nanuet, N.Y.: Philipp Feldheim Publishing, 1972), 21 ff; see also Exodus 16:22-30; 35:3.

3. See the commentary on this passage by Niels-Erik A. Andreasen, *The Christian Use of Time* (Nashville, Tenn.: Abingdon, 1978), 38–41.

4. See Niels-Erik A. Andreasen, *The Old Testament Sabbath: A Tradition-Historical Investigation*, Dissertation Series, no. 7 (Missoula, Mont.: Society of Biblical Literature, 1972).

5. See G. van der Leeuw, *Religion in Essence and Manifestation: A Study in Phenomenology* (Gloucester, Mass.: Peter Smith, 1967), 389.

6. *Oxford Dictionary of the Christian Church*, s.v. "sabbath." ed. F. L. Cross (London: Oxford University Press, 1957).

Chapter 3: The New Covenant and the Early Church

1. For elaboration of this position, see Oscar Cullmann, "Jesus and the Day of Rest," in *Early Christian Worship*, trans. A. Stewart Todd and James B. Torrance (London: SCM Press, 1953).

2. See Samuele Bacchiocchi, *From Sabbath to Sunday: A Historical Investigation of the Rise of Sunday Observance in Early Christianity* (Rome, Italy: Pontifical Gregorian University Press, 1977), 368–69.

3. There is some evidence, however, that Greeks and Romans kept the planetary "Saturn's Day," the same day as the Jewish sabbath, with similar customs. See Willy Rordorf, *Sunday: The History of the Day of Rest and Worship in the Earliest Centuries of the Christian Church*, trans. A. A. K. Graham (Philadelphia, Pa.: Westminster Press, 1968), 29.

4. See Bacchiocchi, *From Sabbath to Sunday*, 301.

5. Marion J. Hatchett, *Commentary on the American Prayer Book* (New York: Seabury Press, 1980).

6. See *New Catholic Encyclopedia*, s.v. "Sunday" (New York: McGraw-Hill, 1967), 797.

7. Those predating the first ecumenical Council of Nicaea in C.E. 325.

8. Such spiritualization of the sabbath probably is behind the later liturgical tradition of treating every day as a *feria*, "a festival," even though some days in the calendar were more festive than others.

9. Roger T. Beckwith and Wilfrid Scott, *This Is the Day: The Biblical Doctrine of the Christian Sunday in Its Jewish and Early Church Setting* (Greenwood, S.C.: Attic Press, 1978), 43, 142.

10. Rordorf, *Sunday: The History*, 142.

11. Ibid., 305.

12. See Herbert Saunders, *The Sabbath: Symbol of Creation and Re-Creating* (Plainfield, N.J.: American Sabbath Tract Society, 1970), for a comprehensive Seventh-Day Baptist statement of position.

13. Cited by Gerard Austin, O.P., in a talk to the Baltimore Congress on Liturgy, 1977.

14. Benedicta Ward, trans., *The Sayings of the Desert Fathers* (Kalamazoo, Mich.: Cistercian Publications, 1975), 12.

Chapter 4: The Later Church

1. An insight of Harry Boone Porter in *The Day of Light: The Biblical and Liturgical Meaning of Sunday* (Greenwich, Conn.: Seabury Press, 1960), 26.

2. Ambrose, Exam. III, 1, 1 (cited in Bacchiocchi, *From Sabbath to Sunday*, 8).

3. Porter, *The Day of Light*, 22.

4. J. Edgar Park, "The Book of Exodus," in *The Interpreter's Bible*, vol. 1 (Nashville, Tenn.: Abingdon, 1952), 984.

5. James Hastings, "Sunday," in *Encyclopaedia of Religion and Ethics* (New York: Scribner, 1951), 106.

6. Rordorf, *Sunday: The History*, 302, and Solberg, *Redeem the Time*, 16.

7. Cited in Solberg, *Redeem the Time*, 198.

8. Ibid.

9. *Oxford Dictionary of the Christian Church*, s.v. "Sabbatarianism."

10. See Solberg, *Redeem the Time*.

11. Ibid., 259.

12. Ibid., 300.

13. Ibid., 300 ff.

14. Special dispensations granted temporarily by the Holy See for doing something not normally permitted.

15. *New Catholic Encyclopedia*, s.v. "Sunday."

16. Ibid., 802.

17. From paragraph 106 of the Liturgical Constitution.

18. See part 3 for some examples.

19. Cited in Roy Branson, "Sabbath—Heart of Jewish Unity," *Journal of Ecumenical Studies* 15, no. 4 (Fall 1978).

Chapter 5: Erosion of the Sabbath

1. I am indebted to Christopher Kiesling, O.P., for stimulating some of these insights in *The Future of the Christian Sunday* (New York: Sheed and Ward, 1970). Other works encountered that deal with the contemporary Sunday situation include: Don Postema, *Catch Your Breath: God's Invitation to Sabbath Rest* (Grand Rapids, Mich.: CRC Publications, 1997); Wayne Muller, *Sabbath: Finding Rest, Renewal, and Delight in Our Busy Lives* (New York: Bantam Books, 2000); Donna Schaper, *Sabbath Keeping* (Cambridge, Mass.: Cowley Publications, 1999); Niels-Erik A. Andreasen, *The Christian Use of Time* (Nashville, Tenn.: Abingdon, 1978); Marva J. Dawn, *Keeping the Sabbath Wholly: Ceasing, Resting, Embracing, Feasting* (Grand Rapids, Mich.: W. B. Eerdmans Publishing Co., 1989); Karen Burton Mains, *Making Sunday Special* (Waco, Tex.: Word Books, 1987); "The Lord's Day," *Liturgy* 8, no. 1 (Summer 1989).

2. See F. W. Dillistone, "Symbolic Stages in Time," in *Traditional Symbols and the Contemporary World* (London: Epworth Press, 1973).

3. Ibid., 118.

4. The exercises and theoretical base are found in the Tibetan Buddhist Lama Tarthang Tulku's *Time, Space, and Knowledge* (Emeryville, Calif.: Dharma Publishing, 1977).

5. I have suggested methods for such practice in past books, with a few additions in part 4.

6. Augustine, *The City of God*, trans. Marcus Dods (New York: Modern Library, 1950), XIX: 19.

7. Cited in Robert Bellah, "To Kill and Survive or To Die and Become: The Active Life and Contemplative Life as Ways of Being Adult," in Erik H. Erikson, ed.,

Adulthood (New York: Norton, 1978), 74. I am indebted to Bellah in my discussion of active and contemplative.

8. Ibid., 75.

9. Ibid., 76.

10. From the essay "Action and Contemplation," in Jacques Maritain's *Scholasticism and Politics* (New York: Arno Press), 192–3.

Chapter 6: Rhythm of Life

1. Icons are sacred Christian paintings through which God and the company of heaven (saints and angels) are venerated, especially in Eastern Orthodox tradition.

2. A twofold human relationship to God described by Gregory of Nyssa, an early church father. It has many later theological variations.

3. See Teresa of Ávila, *Interior Castle*, vol. 2 of *The Complete Works of Saint Teresa of Jesus*, trans. and ed. E. Allison Peers (New York: Sheed and Ward, 1946), 338.

4. See Gabriel, *The Spiritual Director According to the Principles of St. John of the Cross* (Westminster, Md.: Newman, 1950).

5. See Evelyn Eaton Whitehead and James D. Whitehead, *Christian Life Patterns: The Psychological Challenges and Religious Invitations of Adult Life* (Garden City, N.Y.: Doubleday, 1979), 152.

6. BEING/DOING: "The stopping of *doing* on Sunday represents an experience of being saved by grace. It is the renunciation of attempts to work out our own salvation, and our acknowledgment that God is the author and finisher of our faith." (Bacchiocchi, *From Sabbath to Sunday*, 319.)

7. RACHEL/LEAH: Imagery elaborated by Richard of Saint Victor in the twelfth century. See *Richard of St. Victor: The Twelve Patriarchs, the Mystical Ark, Book Three of the Trinity*, trans. Grover A. Zinn (New York: Paulist Press, 1979).

8. CONTEMPLATIVE/ACTIVE: Cassian and others in the early church divided these as different *ways* of life: the *active* being pursuit of virtue, leading to an ordered and recollected life that may or may not involve service to others; the *contemplative* being the pursuit of the higher states of spiritual awareness, building on the discipline of the active life. With a person like Ignatius of Loyola in the sixteenth century, we move toward a systematic justification for the complementarity and interpenetration of contemplation and service to others in *one* way of life, to "seeing God in all things."

9. DETACHMENT/ATTACHMENT: Friedrich von Hügel (along with other classic and modern mystics) says that a person who alternates between detachment and attachment is the one who has the strength which fits him or her for service of others. For von Hügel, that great lay spiritual director of the early twentieth century, periodic detachment keeps the friction between mystical, institutional, and intellectual dimensions of the Christian life from becoming intolerable, and provides the coherence and unity to life that help a person create other moments of total self-outpouring. (See Leonard Biallas, "Von Hügel's Contributions to Religious Studies and to Religion," *Horizons* 6, no. 1 [1979]: 77–78.)

10. INTEGRATION/DISPERSION: One of the great values of an intimate praxis of sabbath and ministry is its capacity to reveal and ease our "dissipated" and "compelled" modes of time. James Whitehead speaks of dissipation as our experience of time as pointless or directionless, and of compulsion as obsessively focused, possessed. Between the extremes lies what he calls "concentration," times when we feel especially present, focused, and gifted. Such times can be called *kairotic,* or fully gifted time, as opposed to mere *chronos,* the experience of time as empty of driven duration. (See James Whitehead, "An Asceticism of Time," *Review for Religious* 39, no. 1 [January/February 1980].)

11. *ANIMA/ANIMUS:* Following Carl Jung, the contemporary Hasidic Rabbi Zalman Schachter speaks of these not in relation to men and women, but as symbols for different modes of being that belong to all of us. Weekdays, he says, our response is masculine: we "husband" the earth and our strength. On the sabbath, though, our response is feminine: we receive and conceive, we are impregnated with a supernal soul, we give birth to tenderness—a rich, warm, empathetic quality toward ourselves and others. (Cited in printed transcribed notes of a talk, "The Sabbath As the Way of the Jewish Person.") Perhaps it is no accident, then, that Hasidic Jews welcome the Sabbath Queen at the start of sabbath. By such respectful and complementary attention to the feminine and masculine in us, they can be *reconciled* instead of slaying each other.

12. ENJOYING GOD/WORKING WITH GOD: Evelyn Underhill refers to this enjoying and working with God as "balanced parts of one full, rich, and surrendered life" in *The Letters of Evelyn Underhill,* ed. Charles Williams (London: Longmans, Green & Co., 1943).

13. USELESS/USEFUL: A. M. Allchin speaks of the relation of solitude to uselessness/aloneness-with-everybody of the cross and the tomb. Seemingly "useless" time is thereby sanctified; indeed, it is the means of reconciliation. (*The World Is a Wedding: Explorations in Christian Spirituality* (New York: Oxford University Press, 1978), 118–119.

14. ROOT/BRANCHES: Allchin quotes the Welsh poet Waldo Williams: "What is understanding? To find the one root under the branches." (Ibid., 154)

15. DESERT/CITY: Church history has been read as a dialectic between the desert and the city, the flight from one to the other, the finding of one in the other. See *The Desert and the City* by modern Jesuits Thomas M. Gannon and George W. Traub (New York: Macmillan, 1969).

16. PLAY/WORK: Walter Ong speaks of humans as the result of God's free play. When we truly participate in God's freedom, our activity is like the germinal, undifferentiated activity of a child, which is both work and play, both serious application and spontaneous activity for its own sake. Thus only those who "become as little children" can enter God's kingdom. If work is truly human work, it, like play, comes from within, as an effusion of activity spilling out from its immanent source. (Hugo Rahner, preface to *Man at Play: or Did You Ever Practice Eutrapelia?,* trans. Brian Battershaw and Edward Quinn [New York: Herder and Herder, 1967].) Karl Barth says of the sabbath: "On this day [we] are to celebrate, rejoice,

and be free, to the glory of God. . . . This *precedes* talk of work—we must hear the gospel before we can understand the law. . . . We can't value and do justice to work except in the light of its boundary, its solemn interruption—the true time from which alone we can have other [work] time" (*Church Dogmatics*, vol. 3 [Edinburgh: T. & T. Clark, 1936], pt. 4).

17. CENTER/BORDER: "All truth is the center of an intense light losing itself gradually in utter darkness. . . . The mind, when weary of "border work," sinks back upon its center, its home of peace and light, and thence gains fresh conviction and courage to again face the twilight and dark. Force [such a mind] to commit itself absolutely to any border distinction, or force it to shift its home or to restrain its roamings, and you have done your best to endanger its faith and to ruin its happiness. . . . The center is to penetrate every part as salt and yeast" (Friedrich von Hügel [New York: Newman, 1971], 28, 77).

18. INSPIRATION/EXPIRATION: "The spirit of God breathes us out from Himself that we may love, and may do good works; and again He draws us into Himself, that we may rest in fruition. And this is Eternal Life." (Jan van Ruysbroeck, *De Septem Gradibus Amoris*, cap. xiv, cited in Evelyn Underhill, *Mysticism: A Study in the Nature and Development of Man's Spiritual Consciousness* 5th ed. [London: Methuen & Co. Ltd, 1914], 521).

Chapter 7: Sabbath Rest

1. A phrase of Abraham Joshua Heschel in *The Sabbath: Its Meaning for Modern Man* (New York: Farrar, Straus and Young, 1951).

2. Grunfeld, *The Sabbath*, 20.

3. Philo in *De Cherubim*, 87–90, cited in Beckwith and Scott, *This Is the Day*, 11.

4. *Spiritual Friend*, chap. 3.

5. Schachter, "The Sabbath As the Way of the Jewish Person."

6. Ben-Zion Gold, "The Sabbath as the Way of the Law" (reprinted talk).

7. Grunfeld, *The Sabbath*, 6.

8. Ibid., 72.

9. Barth, *Church Dogmatics*, vol. 3, pt. 4, 58, 65.

10. Ibid., 51, 68.

11. Ibid., 67.

12. Harvey Gallagher Cox, "Meditation and Sabbath," chap. 5 in *Turning East: The Promise and Peril of the New Orientalism* (New York: Simon and Schuster, 1977).

13. *Living Simply through the Day: Spiritual Survival in a Complex Age* (New York: Paulist Press, 1977).

14. See Hugo Rahner, *Conference of the Fathers*, 4, 93. The book provides insightful reflection on this virtue, as well as on the whole subject of Christian play. I am indebted to Rahner for greatly assisting my historical understanding of divine/human play.

15. Ibid., 9, 93.

16. Ibid., 28.

17. P. Lersch, cited in *Conference of the Fathers*, 35.

18. Ibid., 29.

19. Cited in the *Yoga Journal* (May–June, 1980): 8.

20. *Meister Eckhart: A Modern Translation*, trans. Raymond Bernard Blakney (New York: Harper & Brothers, 1941), 245, fragment 36.

21. Cited in Rahner, *Man at Play*, 77.

22. Ibid., 89.

23. Ibid., 84.

24. Marilyn Daniels, *The Dance in Christianity* (New York: Paulist Press, 1981).

25. Carla De Sola has a handbook of dance and prayer, with dance related to liturgical seasons, scripture, and special occasions. One is the probably authentic Shaker circle dance for "Simple Gifts." *The Spirit Moves* (Washington, D.C.: The Liturgical Conference, 1977).

26. Zalman Schachter, "The Physiology of the Sabbath," *Healing in Our Time: A Journal of the Sufi Healing Order* 1, no. 1 (Spring/Summer 1981).

27. See chapter 15 for more on rites of passage.

Chapter 8: Sabbath Worship

1. Basil Pennington, a monk of St. Joseph's Abbey in Spencer, Mass.

2. Hatchett, *Commentary on the American Prayer Book*.

3. Kallistos (Timothy) Ware, *The Orthodox Church* (Baltimore, Md.: Penguin Books, 1963), 270–72.

4. The Eucharistic Prayer options in the 1979 Episcopal Book of Common Prayer are a contemporary example.

5. Ware, *The Orthodox Church*, 261.

6. Philip Sherrard, "The Art of the Icon," in *Sacrament and Image: Essays in the Christian Understanding of Man*, A. M. Allchin, ed. (London: The Fellowship of St. Alban and St. Sergius, 1967), 58. For further understanding of icons, see John Baggley, *Doors of Perception: Icons and Their Spiritual Significance* (New York: St. Vladimir's Press, 1988), and Tilden Edwards, *Living in the Presence: Disciplines for the Spiritual Heart* (San Francisco: Harper & Row, 1987), chap. 4.

7. Sherrard, "Art of the Icon," 67. Also, Metropolitan Anthony Bloom, *Living Prayer* (Springfield, Ill.: Templegate Publishers, 1968), 68.

8. Ibid., 68–69.

9. Icons of many contemporary figures have been made by Robert Lentz. Catalog available from Bridge Building Images, Inc., P.O. Box 1048, Burlington, VT 05402-1048. Web site: www.bridgebuilding.com.

10. Barth, *Church Dogmatics*, vol. 3, pt. 4, 54, 62–64.

Chapter 10: Social Implications of Sabbath Time

1. The first five books of the Bible.

2. Rordorf, *Sunday: The History*, 12.

3. Lowell, quoted by R. H. Martin in *The Day* (Pittsburgh, Pa.: Office of the National Reform Association, 1933), 179.

4. Hallam, cited in Martin, *The Day*, 184.

5. Cited by Gabe Huck in *Keeping Sunday Holy*, a cassette of the *National Catholic Reporter*, Kansas City, Mo.

6. Ibid.

Chapter 12: Sources and Differences

1. Whitehead, *Christian Life Patterns*.

2. Barth, *Church Dogmatics*, 72.

3. Director of the Catholic-Jewish Relations Office of the National Catholic Conference of Bishops; lecture given to a Memphis interfaith conference on the family, reported in the May 16, 1980, issue of the *National Catholic Reporter*.

Chapter 13: Preparation and Saturday Evening

1. Huck, *Keeping Sunday Holy*.

2. Beckwith and Scott, *This Is the Day*, 43.

3. The research was done by two Dutch psychologists, Ad Vingerhoets and Maaike van Huijgevoort, and presented to the American Psychosomatic Society; cited in the "Intake" column of the *Washington Post*, 27 March 2001.

4. Porter, *The Day of Light*, 78.

5. I am indebted to the Rev. Almus Thorpe Jr. for this information, based on his sabbatical newsletter in the fall of 1980.

6. Gabe Huck, *A Book of Family Prayer* (New York: Seabury, 1979), 51. I am indebted to this layman, the former head of the National Roman Catholic Liturgical Conference, for his pioneering work in recognizing the value of sabbath practices for Christians today.

7. Edward Hays, *Prayers for the Domestic Church: A Handbook for Worship in the Home* (Leavenworth, Kans.: Forest of Peace Publishing, 1979), 86.

8. Quoted from a church bulletin article by Phyllis Bernard Robison.

9. David de Sola Pool, ed. and trans., *The Traditional Prayer Book for Sabbath and Festivals* (New Hyde Park, N.Y.: University Books, 1960), 29.

10. Ibid., 42.

11. Heschel, *The Sabbath*, 59.

12. This is a slight variation of a suggestion by Huck, *A Book of Family Prayer*, 2.

13. Ibid., 52–53.

14. Hays, *Prayers for the Domestic Church*, 87.

15. Mains, *Making Sunday Special*, 48.

16. See De Sola, *The Spirit Moves*.

Chapter 14: Sunday Morning

1. See Gordon S. Wakefield, *Puritan Devotion: Its Place in the Development of Christian Piety* (London: Epworth Press, 1957).

2. The exhortation of a third-century bishop in the *Didascalia Apostolorum* is an example of the great weight given to the corporate nature of the day in the early church, especially in the Eucharist. "Be faithful to the gathering," he says. "Don't deprive the body of one of its members." Gerard Austin speaks of our collective time then as "re-creating" the church, continuing Jesus' Paschal Mystery by our corporate involvement in the bread and wine.

3. I am indebted to Dr. Krister Stendahl of the Harvard Divinity School for stimulating this insight and information about the Swedish Church. More informal base communities are increasingly popular among Roman Catholics today, especially in Latin America. Some Protestant churches have their own versions of these.

Chapter 15: Sunday Afternoon and Closure

1. A reality corroborated by Rabbi Zalman Schachter in Jewish practice as well.

2. Andreasen, *The Christian Use of Time*, 108.

3. *Richard of St. Victor*, trans. Zinn.

4. For detailed contemplative practices appropriate for sabbath, see my books *Living Simply through the Day* and *Living in the Presence*.

5. Huck, *A Book of Family Prayer*, 56.

6. Grunfeld, *The Sabbath*, 68.

7. Heschel, *The Sabbath*, 89.

8. This quotation was sent to me without source.

Chapter 16: Times of Passage

1. Pilgrimage as an extended sabbath time is a neglected discipline today. Victor Witter Turner calls it a voluntary means of liberation from profane social structures, a limited experience aimed at intensified religious commitment. He says that pilgrimage has long stood for voluntaristic mobility in a rooted system. In a destabilized system (ours), life has become one long pilgrimage, without map or sacred goal (*Image and Pilgrimage in Christian Culture: Anthropological Perspectives* [New York: Columbia University Press, 1978]). Perhaps this situation lies behind the popularity of books on "life stages" and "spiritual journeys" today. At the same time, a classical sabbath pilgrimage to a holy place at a particular point in life may help give a needed intensive paradigm for the life of pilgrimage. It is interesting to see the enormous response of youth to pilgrimage invitations from the ecumenical Taizé community in eastern France (and several recent American versions of it),

wherein a global vision of shared suffering, justice, reconciliation, and mutual support centered on the risen Christ is held up and witnessed.

2. "When the body sleeps, the soul is enfolded in One." Thomas Merton, *The Way of Chuang-Tzu* (New York: New Directions, 1965), 40.

3. The church year marks the primary passages of Jesus' life for us, along with the passage of scriptural and historical saints worthy of "resting with" for a while.

4. See James W. Fowler's fourth stage of faith development in *Life Maps* by Fowler and Sam Keen and ed. Jerome Berryman (Waco, Tex.: Word, 1978), 69 ff.

5. Hans Lietzmann, *The Founding of the Church Universal* 2d. ed., trans. Bertram Lee Woolf (New York: Scribner, 1950).

6. See, for example, Turner, *Image and Pilgrimage in Christian Culture.*

7. The art of dying as a Christian is again being taken seriously. One classic on this subject is Jeremy Taylor's seventeenth-century *Holy Dying*. A more contemporary resource is Nathan R. Kollar's *Death and Other Living Things* (Dayton, Ohio: Pflaum Press, 1973).

8. The German philosopher Josef Pieper's penetrating classic essay "Leisure, the Basis of Culture" would be valuable background reading for anyone wanting to further understand the meaning of leisure in Western religious experience, especially the relation of leisure, culture, festival, and worship.

Conclusion: The Rest of Labor and Love

1. Jan van Ruysbroeck, *The Adornment of the Spiritual Marriage.* Cited in Thomas S. Kepler, comp., *An Anthology of Devotional Literature* (Grand Rapids, Mich.: Baker Book House, 1977), 194.

2. Ibid.

About the Author

Tilden Edwards is the founder and senior fellow of the Shalem Institute for Spiritual Formation in Bethesda, Maryland. An ecumenical Christian organization, The Shalem Institute offers extension programs, retreats, workshops, and media resources for laity and clergy. Edwards is the author of numerous books and articles on various aspects of spiritual formation and is widely recognized as one of the most influential writers in the field.

Don't miss these Upper Room titles!

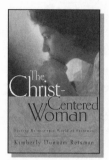

The Christ-Centered Woman
Finding Balance in a World of Extremes
BY KIMBERLY DUNNAM REISMAN

Christian women must respond to many callings—those of family and home, work and colleagues, ministry and discipleship. In this insightful guide, Kimberly Dunnam Reisman confronts the daily chaos of competing demands from a new perspective. She does not ask, "How do I juggle my responsibilities?" but instead asks, "How do I make choices that reflect my relationship with Christ and Christ's direction for my life?" Reisman, a graduate of Emory University and Yale Divinity School, is associate pastor of Trinity United Methodist Church in Lafayette, Indiana. She is also a wife and mother of three.

ISBN 0-8358-0913-7 • Paperback • 112 pages

Living in God's Time
A Parent's Guide to Nurturing Children throughout the Christian Year
BY MARGARET MCMILLAN PERSKY

Every parent is really a potter—one who molds and shapes. *Living in God's Time* shows parents how to intentionally mold into their children a daily awareness of God. Christian educator Margaret McMillan Persky takes the reader through the Christian year by explaining the foundational importance of each season to our inner rhythms of spiritual growth. Through *Living in God's Time*, parents and children alike learn to reflect daily on God's movement in daily life and to consider who and whose they are.

ISBN 0-8358-0875-0 • Paperback • 144 pages

Quiet Spaces
Prayer Interludes for Women
BY PATRICIA WILSON

The intimate relationship with God you have yearned for is well within your grasp, despite the chaos of juggling multiple roles, deadlines, and commitments. With *Quiet Spaces*, you can learn to calm your mind and to listen for God's still small voice in the midst of the tumult around you.

Through this book, Patricia Wilson shows how even a few stray minutes can become a blessed opportunity for a focused encounter with God. Each prayer interlude, which can be completed in as few as five minutes, offers a calming passage from the Psalms, a heartfelt prayer, inspiration from Christ's words, and an exercise to help readers return to their world.

ISBN 0-8358-0969-2• Paperback • 224 pages

Journaling
A Spiritual Journey (Revised Edition)
BY ANNE BROYLES

Unlike most books, which are either a journal or a book about journaling, *Journaling* is both. It contains helpful suggestions for journaling and sufficient space to practice each method. The methods include journaling from the events of daily life, journaling in response to scripture, journaling with guided meditations, journaling from dreams, journaling in response to reading, and journaling conversations or dialogues.

Appropriate for individuals or small groups, this book will enable journalers to reflect on their relationship with God and receive insights to aid them in their spiritual walk.

ISBN 0-8358-0866-1 • Paperback • 144 pages